Outdoor Recreation
in the Northern United States

H. Ken Cordell, Carter J. Betz, Shela H. Mou, and Dale D. Gormanson

H. KEN CORDELL, PIONEERING RESEARCH SCIENTIST
Southern Research Station, U.S. Forest Service
320 Green Street
Athens, GA 30602
706-559-4263
kcordell@fs.fed.us

CARTER J. BETZ
Formerly with Southern Research Station
U.S. Forest Service
1280 Robinhood Road
Watkinsville, GA 30677
706-769-8437
carterbetz@bellsouth.net

SHELA H. MOU, COMPUTER ASSISTANT
Southern Research Station, U.S. Forest Service
320 Green Street
Athens, GA 30602
706-559-4262
smou@fs.fed.us

DALE D. GORMANSON, FORESTER
Northern Research Station, U.S. Forest Service
1992 Folwell Avenue
St. Paul, MN 55108
651-649-5126
dgormanson@fs.fed.us

i

C O N T E N T S

Outdoor Recreation in the Northern United States

INTRODUCTION

This publication is part of the Northern Forest Futures Project, through which the Northern Research Station of the U.S. Forest Service examines the issues, trends, threats, and opportunities facing the forests of the northern United States. It complements the *Forests of the Northern United States* (Shifley et al. 2012) which summarizes forest-related concerns that are unique to the northern United States and discusses characteristics associated with forest sustainability in the region.

This publication is intended for natural resource managers and planners, policy makers, State natural resource agencies, politicians, students, and those who want to know more about recreation in northern forests.

In this report, we describe recent population trends and forecasts for the North within the context of other U.S. regions, demographic composition of its population, recreation participation by its residents age 16 and older, trends in activities and time spent outdoors by its youth, and the recreation resources, both public and private. The region referenced here includes the 20 states bounded by the corner states of Maine, Minnesota, Missouri, and Maryland.

Much of the research reported here ties to data, analyses, and findings developed for the U.S. Department of Agriculture Forest Service 2010 Renewable Resources Planning Act (RPA) Assessment (Cordell 2012). The data and methods employed are described in the appendix at the end of this report. The Forest and Rangeland Renewable Resources Planning Act of 1974 mandated a decennial national assessment (with periodic updates) of the renewable resources on all public and private forest and range ownerships. Each RPA Assessment provides a snapshot of current conditions and trends on U.S. forest and range lands, identifies factors that drive change, and makes model-driven 50-year projections of demands, uses, and conditions for recreation, water, timber, wildlife (biodiversity), and urban-forest and range resources. Trends and forecasts in land use and climate change are also included. The 2010 RPA Assessment stresses the influence of climate change on forest and grassland resources and has adapted three socioeconomic scenarios based on the fourth world assessment of climate change (Intergovernmental Panel on Climate Change 2007). RPA population forecasts to 2060 based on these three scenarios are reported later in this report. The 2010 set of special RPA resource studies (which include 2060 forecasts) and the national summary are in press.

It was not until the post-World War II years that a number of social and economic forces combined to make outdoor recreation a national phenomenon that required serious attention and study. Three of the major forces at work included rising real incomes, the proliferation of automobiles and highways (especially the Interstate Highway System), and increasing leisure as the United States continued shifting from a predominantly agricultural to a manufacturing and service-based economy. Increasingly, in the 1950s and 1960s, Americans took to the open road to see and experience "the great outdoors." A direct result was mounting pressures on recreation facilities and most public lands (Clawson and Knetsch 1966, Cordell 2012). Consequently, major efforts were undertaken beginning in the late 1950s to better understand Americans' growing interest in outdoor recreation. Most notable was the Outdoor Recreation Resources Review Commission, established by Congress in 1958 to conduct a comprehensive nationwide assessment of outdoor recreation conditions and trends.

Interest in monitoring outdoor recreation trends continues to the present day (Cordell 2008). In an earlier national report, we reported that Americans' participation in outdoor activities, including nature-based recreation activities, had been increasing up through the first few years of the 2000s (Cordell et al. 2004).

Many Americans love to visit the "great outdoors"
such as the Presidential Range in the White Mountains
National Forest of New Hampshire.
(Photograph by Bob Ward)

Overall, since the commission released its report (Outdoor Recreation Resources Review Commission 1962), many forms of outdoor activity and public land visitation have been observed to be growing and diversifying:

Both the NSRE (National Survey on Recreation and the Environment) and the National Survey on Fishing, Hunting, and Wildlife-Associated Recreation show that participation in some nature-based activities has declined. However, for many other activities there seems to be growing popularity. Some outdoor recreation activities have even demonstrated rather strong popularity growth. One such activity is visiting wilderness and other primitive areas. (Cordell et al. 2008)

Because trends in outdoor recreation have far reaching implications for both people and natural resources, a close look at those trends and projected futures for the Northern States is an important part of the Northern Forest Futures Project, currently underway at the Forest Service (Northern Research Station, Eastern Region, Forest Products Laboratory, and Northeastern Area State and Private Forestry) in partnership with the Northeastern Area Association of State Foresters and the University of Missouri.

Outdoor recreation can take many forms depending on the types of activities, settings, social engagements, equipment, and times chosen by the recreation participant. Recreation can be physically active (for example, hiking) or more sedentary (for example, viewing natural scenery). Many of the activities of interest to the RPA Assessment and to assessments of current or future northern forest conditions are classified as "nature-based" in that they are in some way associated with wildlife, birds, streams, lakes, snow and ice areas, trails, rugged terrain, mountains, caves, and other natural outdoor resources or settings. For example, included among our list of nature-based activities are mountain biking, coldwater fishing, whitewater rafting, downhill skiing, primitive camping, backpacking, mountain climbing, visiting prehistoric sites, saltwater fishing, and snorkeling. Nature-based recreation participation is summarized for the North across seven activity groups:

- **Visiting recreation and historic sites—** Visiting the beach, visiting prehistoric sites, visiting historic sites, developed camping, swimming in lakes/ponds/streams, and visiting watersides (besides beaches)
- **Viewing/photographing nature—**Viewing/ photographing birds, fish, other wildlife, natural scenery, wildflowers/trees/other plants, visiting nature centers, sightseeing, gathering mushrooms/berries, and participating in boat tours or excursions
- **Backcountry activities—**Backpacking, day hiking, horseback riding on trails, mountain climbing, visiting a wilderness or primitive area, primitive camping, mountain biking, caving, rock climbing, and orienteering

- **Motorized activities**—Motorboating, off-highway-vehicle driving (four-wheel-drive vehicle, all-terrain vehicle, or motorcycle), snowmobiling, using personal watercraft, and waterskiing

- **Hunting and fishing**—Anadromous fishing (salt-to-fresh-water migratory fish such as salmon), coldwater fishing, warmwater fishing, saltwater fishing, big game hunting, small game hunting, and migratory bird hunting

- **Non-motorized boating and diving**—Canoeing, kayaking, rafting, rowing, sailing, surfing, windsurfing, snorkeling, and scuba diving

- **Snow skiing and other winter activities**—Cross country skiing, downhill skiing, snowboarding, snowshoeing, and ice fishing

SNOW-SHOE TRAIL

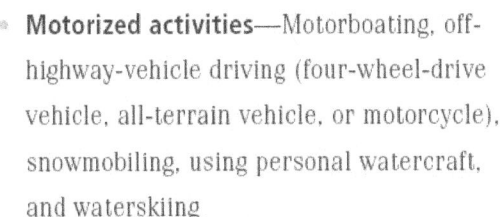

Population and Demographic Trends
CURRENT POPULATION TRENDS FOR THE NORTH

Race and ethnic composition data from the U.S. Department of Commerce, Bureau of the Census, along with the percentage change trends from 1990 to 2009, are summarized by region in Table 1. Race and ethnicity are important determinants of what people choose as outdoor recreation activities and the settings they prefer for those activities. For example, African Americans tend to participate much less frequently in wildland recreation activities and many Hispanics appear to prefer settings that will accommodate large-group activities such as picnicking (Cordell et al. 2004).

Table 1—Population in 2009 by race/ethnicity and region, and change since 1990 (Source: U.S. Department of Commerce, Bureau of the Census 1990, 2009a).

Race / ethnicity	North		South		Rocky Mountains		Pacific Coast		United States	
	Population (thousands)	Change (percent)	Population (thousands)	Change (percent)	Population (thousands)	Change (percent)	Population (thousands)	Change (percent)	Population (thousands)	Change (percent)
Non-Hispanic White	92,333.8	-0.2	63,761.3	14.6	19,544.5	25.7	24,211.7	-1.7	199,851.2	6.1
African American	14,899.9	19.7	19,202.6	37.9	998.6	77.6	2,580.5	9.3	37,681.5	28.6
American Indian	421.7	24.7	716.4	38.8	779.5	40.2	443.2	14.7	2,360.8	31.4
Asian or Pacific Islander	4,806.0	122.7	2,626.0	186.4	732.2	187.4	5,970.4	62.9	14,134.6	102.0
Two or more races[a]	1,524.1	.	1,311.0	.	442.1	.	1,281.8	.	4,559.0	.
Hispanic[b]	11,064.6	100.1	16,696.6	153.6	5,700.5	167.3	14,957.7	84.0	48,419.3	116.4
Total	125,050.0	10.7	104,313.8	34.4	28,197.5	48.0	49,445.2	26.2	307,006.6	23.4

[a]Percentage change for two or more races is missing because U.S. citizens were not offered the option to select more than one race until the 2000 census.

[b]Hispanics of all races are included in this category.

Demographic changes in the North and throughout the Nation will bring a changing constituency for outdoor recreation and conservation, such as this Maryland group of students working on a schoolyard habitat project. (Photograph by LaVonda Walton)

The changes in the racial and ethnic makeup of the U.S. population have been dramatic since the 1990 census. Although all groups have been growing in number, generally, Hispanics and Asian/Pacific Islanders have been growing fastest. Slowest growing of all the groups has been non-Hispanic Whites. The North had the lowest growth rate and the Rocky Mountains highest. The highest percentage growth of any group since 1990 has been Asians/Pacific Islanders in the Rocky Mountains and South, each with about a 187 percent increase. Non-Hispanic Whites experienced slight population losses in the North and Pacific Coast.

The Rocky Mountains and South are the only regions that exceeded the national rate for all groups. Total population growth in the North was 10.7 percent, less than half the national rate (23.4 percent); this held true for all groups except Asians/Pacific Islanders, which more than doubled in the North since 1990 (122.7 percent). The non-Hispanic White population almost held constant, declining just 0.2 percent. However, the North has the largest share of non-Hispanic Whites (almost 74 percent), which depressed its overall growth rate to less than 11 percent. About 14.9 million African Americans live in the North, 40 percent of the national total; the growth rate for the group was 19.7 percent, compared to 28.6 percent nationally.

Table 2—Population in 2009 by age group and region, and change since 1990 (Source: U.S. Department of Commerce, Bureau of the Census 1990, 2009a).

Age Group	North		South		Rocky Mountains		Pacific Coast		United States	
(years)	Population (thousands)	Change (percent)	Population (thousands)	Change (percent)	Population (thousands)	Change (percent)	Population (thousands)	Change (percent)	Population (thousands)	Change (percent)
<6	9,569.8	-2.3	9,022.6	29.9	2,603.7	40.2	4,289.1	12.9	25,485.2	13.8
6 to 10	7,886.2	0.0	7,151.7	25.4	2,009.3	28.4	3,323.3	14.9	20,370.5	12.9
11 to 15	8,088.2	9.3	6,857.8	27.5	1,893.1	34.2	3,321.7	29.8	20,160.9	20.4
16 to 24	15,725.2	4.2	13,165.7	23.2	3,675.3	47.1	6,377.4	17.4	38,943.7	15.5
25 to 34	16,138.0	-16.6	14,275.9	7.4	3,995.4	23.6	7,157.0	-2.1	41,566.3	-3.7
35 to 44	16,880.1	-0.5	14,126.6	23.2	3,635.1	27.2	6,888.2	11.7	41,530.0	10.9
45 to 54	19,028.4	64.1	14,688.1	88.1	3,856.5	111.0	7,019.5	83.3	44,592.5	77.9
55 to 64	14,740.7	47.0	11,597.0	75.8	3,092.5	102.9	5,356.8	80.5	34,786.9	64.7
≥65	16,993.4	14.4	13,428.4	38.0	3,436.6	51.1	5,712.1	35.3	39,570.6	27.3
Total	125,050.0	10.7	104,313.8	34.4	28,197.5	48.0	49,445.2	26.2	307,006.6	23.4

The North lags behind other regions in American Indian population, although it is a close second to the Pacific Coast and has grown 10 percent faster than that region since 1990.

Only the Pacific Coast has more Asians/Pacific Islanders, whose growth rate was nearly twice as high in the North as the Pacific Coast. The Hispanic population in the North almost exactly doubled, growing to almost 11.1 million.

Age distribution—Age is another important determinant of recreation activity choices (Cordell et al. 2004). Similar to race and ethnicity, the age distribution of the U.S. population has been changing over time (Table 2). The fastest growing age group since 1990 (in percentage change) has been age 45 to 54, followed by age 55 to 64. Third fastest has been age 65 and older. The 45-to-54-age group grew fastest in all regions. In the North, the 25-to-34-age group decreased nearly 17 percent, contributing to a national drop in population of almost 4 percent. The Pacific Coast was the only other region to lose population in this young adult segment. Also losing population in the North was the youngest age group (younger than 6 years). The 6-to-10-age group essentially held constant since 1990. These two youngest segments of the U.S. population grew at double-digit rates in every other region, fastest in the Rocky Mountains.

Similar to the Nation, northern Baby Boomers (ages 45 to 54 and 55 to 64) dominated all other age groups in percentage growth (Table 2), but at a slower rate. However, the North experienced a greater disparity between the two Baby Boomer groups and the third-place age group (age 65 and older) than the Nation as a whole. Percentage growth for the age 55 to 64 group was more than three times that of the oldest age group, and the age 45 to 54 group grew at more than four times the rate of the age 65 and older group. No other region nor the Nation approached these growth rates.

Further, the North has the oldest population of any U.S. region. Almost 41 percent of its residents are age 45 or older; no other region has more than 38 percent in this age group. As with race and ethnicity, the South and Rocky Mountains were the only regions to outpace the national growth rate for every single age group. Conversely, northern populations increased (or decreased) at a slower rate than the Nation in all age groups. The three age groups in the North that lost population include the youngest age group (under 6) and the two groups that spanned age 25 to 44. The number of young adults age 25 to 34 in their prime childbearing years, in particular, decreased at a far greater rate in the North than any other age group in any region. This trend helps explain the decrease and lack of growth in the two youngest age groups. In addition to growing more slowly than the Nation and any other region in total population, the North's modest 11 percent population gain since 1990 occurred overwhelmingly in the three oldest cohorts age 45 and older. A greater share of the northern population appears to be aging-in-place compared to other regions. The decrease in young adult populations in the North is the result of lower birth-to-death rates and of young people seeking economic opportunities elsewhere (Franklin 2003, Yang and Snyder 2007).

Population density—Population density (persons per square mile) is greatest in Florida, in the Piedmont areas of North Carolina to Georgia, along the coast of the northern Atlantic States, in several Great Lakes and midwestern metropolitan areas, in eastern Texas, in the Denver-Front Range area, and in scattered areas along the Pacific Coast and into Arizona (Fig. 1). In Alaska, density is greatest in the Anchorage area.

The North has for years been well known for the cluster of densely populated counties that extend from the Washington-Baltimore metropolitan to southern New Hampshire. Urban or mostly urban counties also stretch almost continuously along the Great Lakes from central New York to Green Bay, WI. Other high-density areas include western Pennsylvania, parts of Ohio, and metropolitan areas around Indianapolis, St. Louis, the Twin Cities of Minneapolis/St. Paul, and Kansas City, MO.

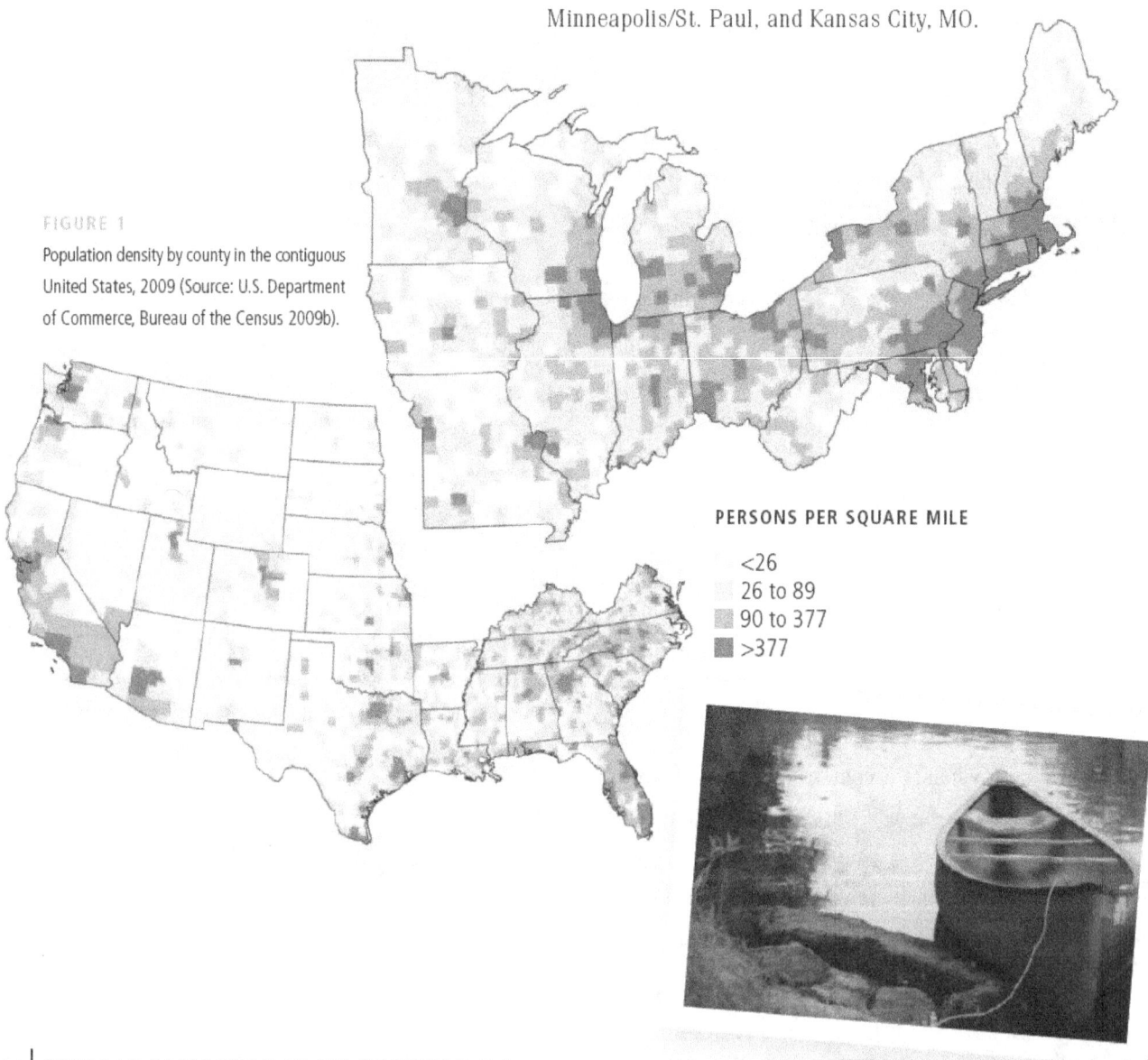

FIGURE 1

Population density by county in the contiguous United States, 2009 (Source: U.S. Department of Commerce, Bureau of the Census 2009b).

PERSONS PER SQUARE MILE

<26
26 to 89
90 to 377
>377

The North has the largest number of counties in the two most densely populated classes (more than 90 persons per square mile); most of its counties in the least densely populated category are located in the midwestern area and northern Maine (Fig. 1).

Figure 2 shows that much of the overall population-density growth in the East has occurred along the northern Atlantic coast, down the Piedmont and Southern Appalachians from North Carolina to greater Atlanta, in peninsular Florida, around Chicago, the Twin Cities, and the major cities of Texas.

Elsewhere in the United States, growth occurred in the Denver and Salt Lake City metropolitan areas, in the Bay Area and southern California areas, and in greater Seattle and Portland, OR. In some areas—such as eastern Texas, metropolitan Atlanta, and Orange County in California—population growth exceeds 500 persons per square mile, which is the U.S. Department of Commerce, Bureau of the Census definition of an urban area. Greater concentrations of people in places near public lands and bodies of water are likely to put increasing pressures on these limited resources.

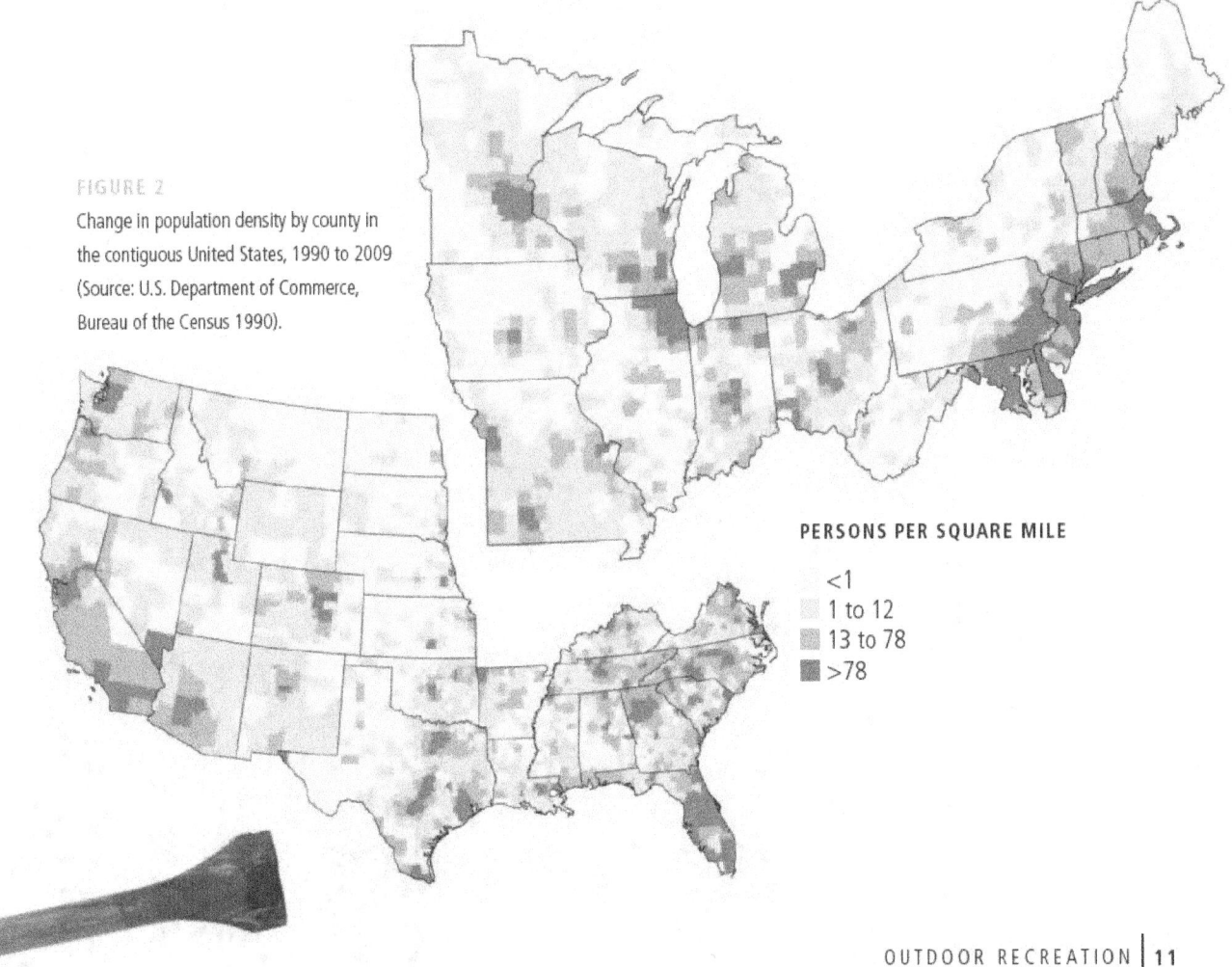

FIGURE 2

Change in population density by county in the contiguous United States, 1990 to 2009 (Source: U.S. Department of Commerce, Bureau of the Census 1990).

PERSONS PER SQUARE MILE

<1
1 to 12
13 to 78
>78

In the North, population density increased the most throughout the Washington-to-Boston urban corridor and also in the greater Chicago and Twin Cities areas. Noticeably different from their high population-density rankings (Fig. 1), few Northern counties are in the two highest growth categories (which represents the top 30 percent of all U.S. counties); this is especially true in Ohio, Michigan, and Indiana. Conversely, more Northern counties (including much of Pennsylvania, West Virginia, New York, Illinois, and Iowa) are in the lowest growth category, which represents a loss or negligible growth in population since 1990. The urban cores of metropolitan Detroit, Cleveland, Cincinnati, St. Louis, and Buffalo, NY, lost population over the 19-year period.

Hispanics—From 1990 to 2009, Hispanic population growth has exceeded 800 percent in some U.S. counties (Fig. 3). Much of the fastest growth has been in the southern States bordering the Atlantic Ocean and Mississippi River. High rates of growth have also occurred through the upper midwestern area and through selected areas of the West. With some exceptions, the rate of Hispanic growth in the North has been lower than most of the South; however, even the second-lowest category represents up to 357 percent growth.

FIGURE 3

Change in Hispanic population of all races by county in the contiguous United States, 1990 to 2009 (source: U.S. Department of Commerce, Bureau of the Census 1990, 2009b)..

PERCENT

<150
150 to 357
358 to 818
>818

Just a few northern counties—in Minnesota, Missouri, West Virginia, and Illinois—have experienced reductions in their Hispanic populations. Very high rates of Hispanic population growth—more than 818 percent in less than 20 years—occurred in Minnesota, Iowa, Missouri, Indiana, and a scattering of counties elsewhere. The lowest rates occurred in Michigan, New York, much of Ohio and Illinois, and the New England States.

Non-Hispanic Whites—The non-Hispanic White population in the United States has been growing in metropolitan areas such as Atlanta, Washington, the Raleigh/Durham area in North Carolina, the Twin Cities, eastern Texas, and throughout much of the West (Fig. 4).

Areas rich in natural amenities—such as the Rocky Mountains, Florida, Arizona, Colorado, Utah, and Nevada—appear to have the fastest growth of non-Hispanic White populations. The top tier of percentage change includes counties that increased more than 40 percent, much lower than the highest level of Hispanic population growth. In the North, these high-growth counties were relatively few, located mostly in suburban areas around major cities. Three other areas with faster growing non-Hispanic White populations that are not highly urbanized, but also possess abundant natural amenities, are the Delmarva Peninsula region in Delaware and Maryland, the Delaware Water Gap area of northeastern Pennsylvania, and southern Missouri.

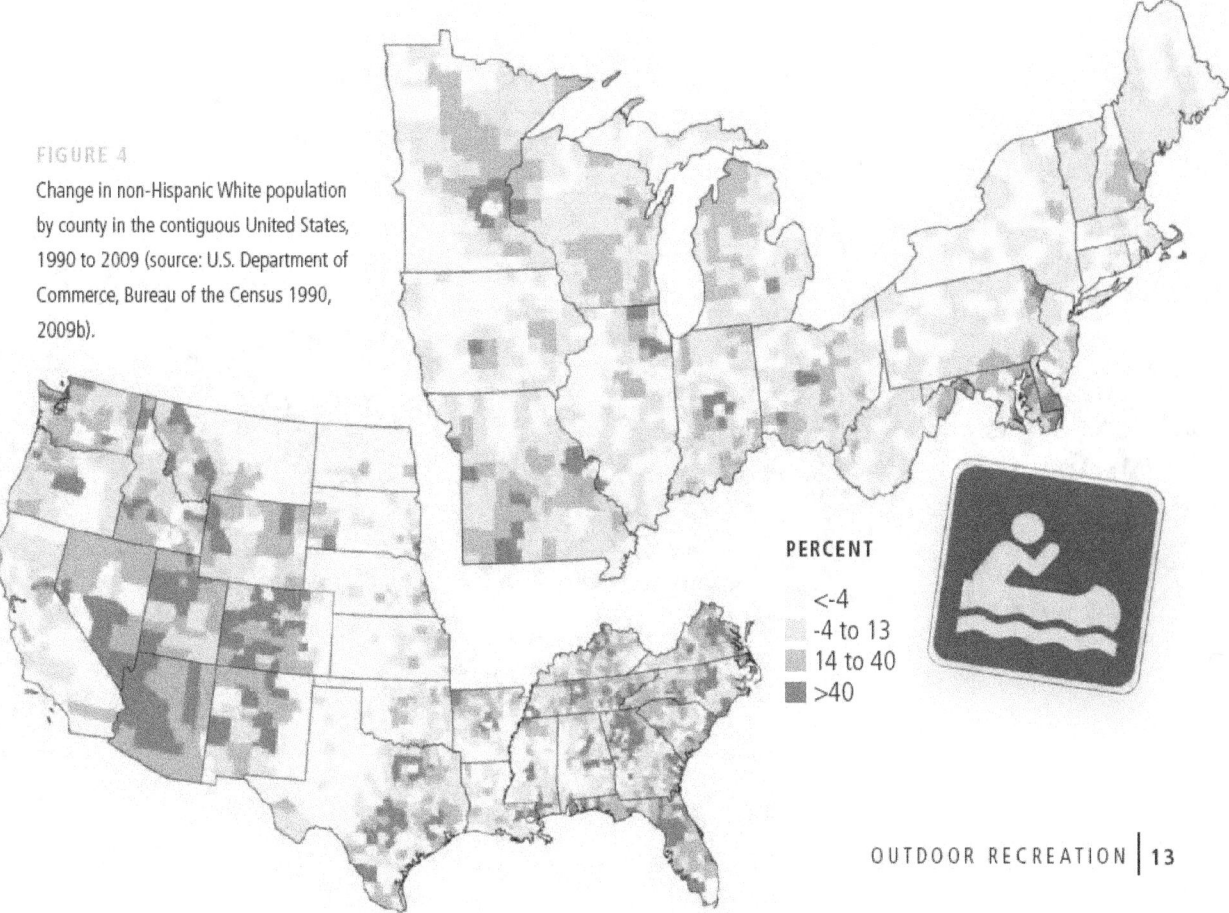

FIGURE 4

Change in non-Hispanic White population by county in the contiguous United States, 1990 to 2009 (source: U.S. Department of Commerce, Bureau of the Census 1990, 2009b).

PERCENT

<-4
-4 to 13
14 to 40
>40

Similar to the trends in population growth and composition since 1990, the regions likely to lead the Nation in projected rate of change under the moderate growth scenario are the Rocky Mountains at 76 percent and the South at 57 percent (Table 3). The Pacific Coast follows closely at 54 percent. The North lags behind the others by a wide margin, with just 26 percent expected growth. The intermountain area of the Rocky Mountains far exceeds all other areas with projected growth of 89 percent (nearly three times the rate of the Great Plains area). By 2060, the South is expected to pass the North as the Nation's most populous region. Currently (2009), the North accounts for 40.7 percent of the total U.S. population, but is projected to drop to 35.2 percent of the total by 2060, compared to 36.6 percent (up from 34.0 percent) in the South, 11.1 percent (up from 9.2 percent) in the Rocky Mountains, and 17.1 percent (up from 16.1 percent) in the Pacific Coast.

The eight States in the north-central area (west of and including Ohio) are projected to grow just slightly faster (26.8 percent) than both the region as a whole (26.0 percent) and the 12 States and the District of Columbia that comprise the northeastern area (25.3 percent). The northeastern area, however, has 7 of the top 10 States ranked by percentage growth, led by New Hampshire, Maryland, and Vermont, each with more than 50 percent projected growth. Minnesota is the only State in the north central area expected to grow more than 50 percent. Ohio, West Virginia, and New York are the three lowest ranking States, each expected to grow less than 13 percent. The District of Columbia is projected to lose almost 17 percent of its population.

Table 3—Estimated population for 2009, projections to 2060 by region and State for three population growth scenarios, and percentage change from 2009 to 2060 for the moderate growth projection (Source: Cordell 2012, U.S. Department of Commerce, Bureau of the Census 2009a).

Region, State	Population 2009	Moderate growth[a] 2060	Change from 2009	High growth[b] 2060	Low growth[c] 2060
	(thousands)	(thousands)	(percent)	(thousands)	(thousands)
Northern States	125,050.0	157,597.9	26.0	178,045.6	139,964.2
Connecticut	3,518.3	4,280.8	21.7	4,836.2	3,801.8
Delaware	885.1	1,308.6	47.8	1,478.4	1,162.2
District of Columbia	599.7	499.7	-16.7	564.5	443.8
Illinois	12,910.4	16,364.5	26.8	18,487.7	14,533.5
Indiana	6,423.1	8,147.5	26.8	9,204.6	7,235.9
Iowa	3,007.9	3,612.9	20.1	4,081.7	3,208.7
Maine	1,318.3	1,755.5	33.2	1,983.2	1,559.0
Maryland	5,699.5	9,120.0	60.0	10,303.3	8,099.5
Massachusetts	6,593.6	7,801.1	18.3	8,813.2	6,928.2
Michigan	9,969.7	12,173.3	22.1	13,752.7	10,811.2
Minnesota	5,266.2	7,987.7	51.7	9,024.1	7,094.0
Missouri	5,987.6	8,091.3	35.1	9,141.1	7,186.0
New Hampshire	1,324.6	2,255.5	70.3	2,548.1	2,003.1
New Jersey	8,707.7	11,969.2	37.5	13,522.2	10,630.0
New York	19,541.5	21,929.1	12.2	24,774.3	19,475.4
Ohio	11,542.6	12,811.1	11.0	14,473.3	11,377.7
Pennsylvania	12,604.8	15,235.9	20.9	17,212.7	13,531.2
Rhode Island	1,053.2	1,403.6	33.3	1,585.7	1,246.6
Vermont	621.8	956.2	53.8	1,080.3	849.3
West Virginia	1,819.8	2,033.8	11.8	2,297.6	1,806.2
Wisconsin	5,654.8	7,860.6	39.0	8,880.5	6,981.1
Southern States	104,313.8	163,673.8	56.9	184,909.9	145,360.3
Rocky Mountains States	28,197.5	49,695.6	76.2	56,143.5	44,135.2
Pacific Coast States	49,445.2	76,340.6	54.4	86,245.5	67,798.9
U.S. total	307,006.6	447,308.0	45.7	505,344.5	397,258.6

a – c: The moderate growth scenario corresponds to mid-range population growth to about 447 million people by 2060, and an average personal income of around $73,000. The high growth scenario projects the highest population growth, reaching more than 505 million and the lowest projected average personal around $50,000. The low growth scenario projects the lowest population growth and mid-level personal income, predicting a population of 397 million people with average personal income around $54,000 by 2060.

Figures 5 through 7 show the geographic patterns of projected changes in population density by 2060—ranging from lowest (fewer than 2 persons per square mile) to the highest (more than 186 persons per square mile)— for the low (Fig. 5), moderate (Fig. 6), and high (Fig. 7) population growth scenarios. For the purposes of this analysis, land area in all counties is assumed to remain constant.

Immediately apparent in the low-growth projection scenario (Fig. 5) is the presence of numerous lower density counties distributed throughout the North, especially throughout much of the midwestern area, New York State, and upper New England. The highest-growth counties, which are expected to add more than 186 persons per square mile, are concentrated mainly in the Washington-to-Boston urban corridor and in other suburban areas throughout the region.

Change in persons per square mile by county in the contiguous United States, 2009 to 2060, for a low growth population projection (Sources: Cordell 2012, U.S. Department of Commerce, Bureau of the Census 2009b). (The low growth scenario projects the lowest population growth and mid-level personal income, predicting a population of 397 million people with average personal income around $54,000 by 2060.)

PERSONS PER SQUARE MILE

<2
2 to 32
33 to 186
>186

The second-tier counties are mostly located around those counties with highest growth, as well as in Michigan, Wisconsin, or southern Missouri.

The moderate growth projection scenario (Fig. 6), which closely approximates the Census Bureau State projections, has fewer low-growth counties, as expected, and more counties in the intermediate ranges (2 to 186 additional persons per square mile). The highest-growth projection scenario mostly adds to the clusters of counties around the major urban centers, especially those in the northeastern area and those near Chicago, Detroit, and the Twin Cities. Under this scenario, very few high-growth counties in the North were added to nonmetropolitan areas high in natural amenities.

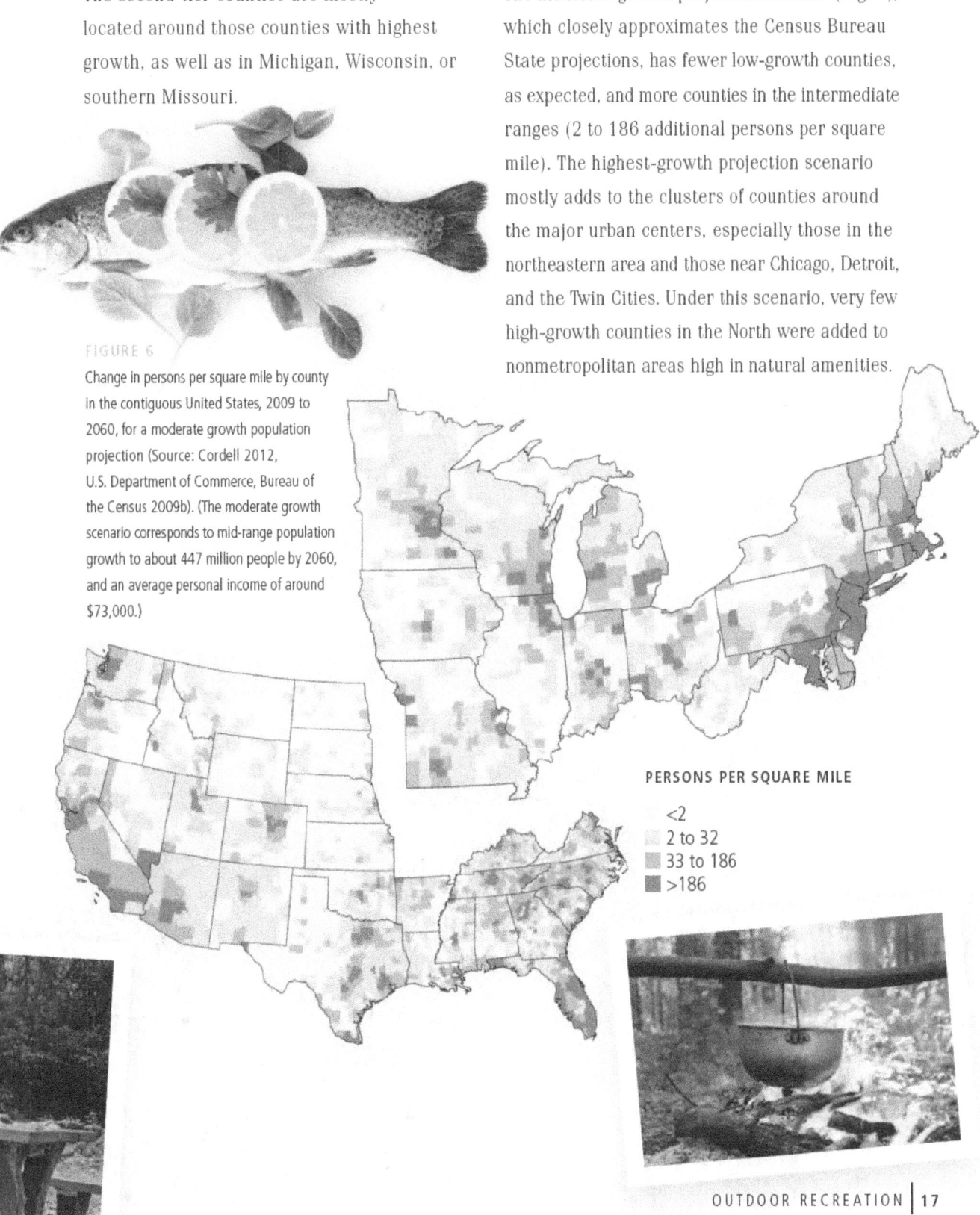

FIGURE 6

Change in persons per square mile by county in the contiguous United States, 2009 to 2060, for a moderate growth population projection (Source: Cordell 2012, U.S. Department of Commerce, Bureau of the Census 2009b). (The moderate growth scenario corresponds to mid-range population growth to about 447 million people by 2060, and an average personal income of around $73,000.)

PERSONS PER SQUARE MILE

<2
2 to 32
33 to 186
>186

Under the high-growth scenario (Fig. 7), more counties shift from the lowest to the two moderate growth categories. The highest growth counties that are expected to add significant population density of more than 186 persons per square mile appear to be limited almost entirely to metropolitan areas, with only a few exceptions. A number of counties scattered throughout the region are projected to remain in the lowest growth class (fewer than 2 persons per square mile added, including population losses), especially in Iowa, northern Missouri and eastward to West Virginia, plus several counties northeastward from Pennsylvania to Maine.

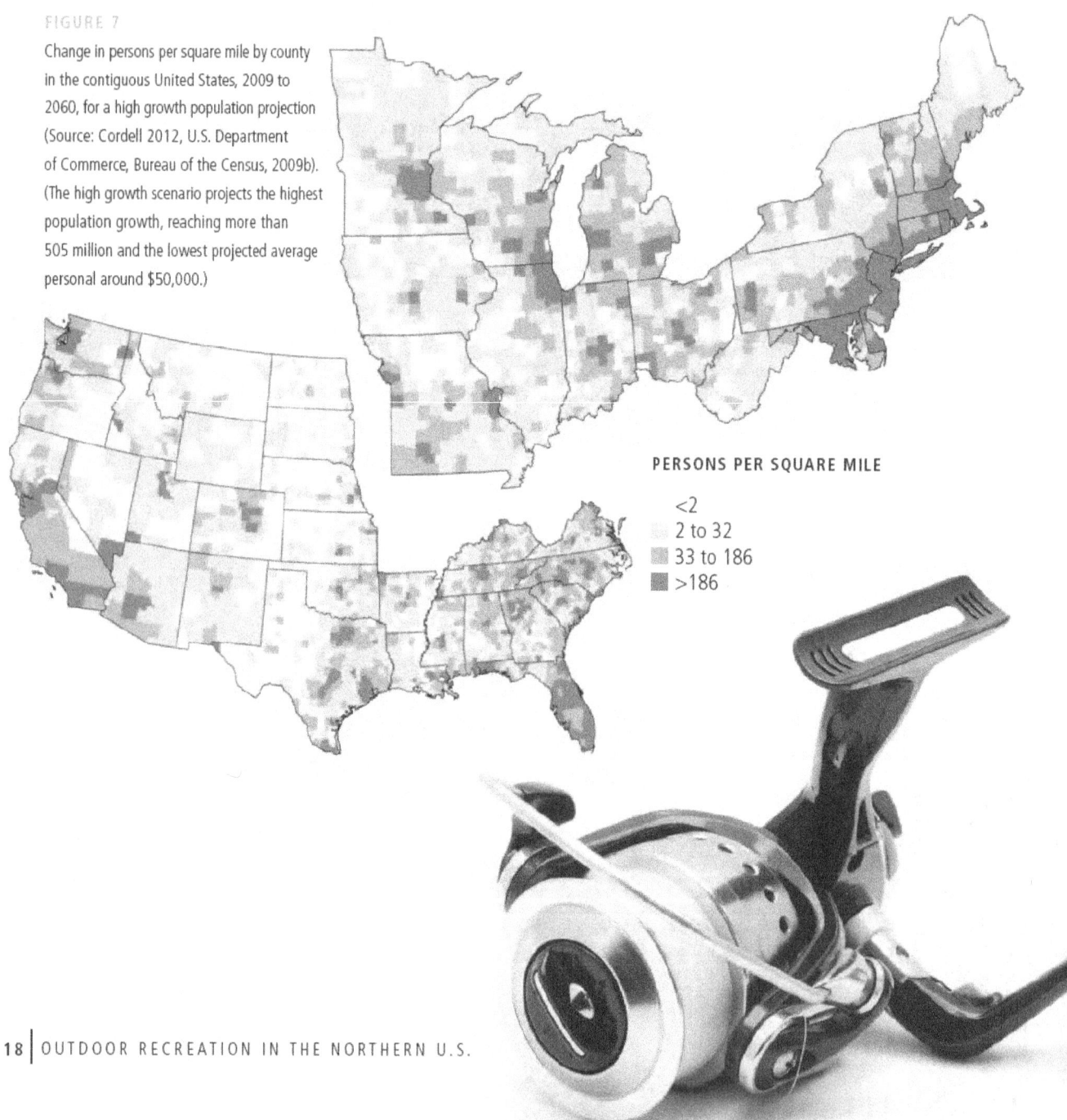

FIGURE 7

Change in persons per square mile by county in the contiguous United States, 2009 to 2060, for a high growth population projection (Source: Cordell 2012, U.S. Department of Commerce, Bureau of the Census, 2009b). (The high growth scenario projects the highest population growth, reaching more than 505 million and the lowest projected average personal around $50,000.)

PERSONS PER SQUARE MILE

<2
2 to 32
33 to 186
>186

Outdoor Recreation Trends

From 1999 to 2009 (single year labels which represent pooled data from the two data collection periods of 1999 to 2001 and 2005 to 2009), the number of people age 16 and older who participated in outdoor recreation grew by 8.5 percent nationally, from an estimated 208.2 million to 226.0 million (Fig. 8).

A participant is anyone who engaged in one or more of 60 outdoor activities during the past 12 months. Included in the list of 60 was a wide range of activities such as attending family gatherings outdoors, viewing wildlife and birds, backpacking, and mountain climbing. Across the range of these activities, the indexed number of total annual activity days of participation (measured as the product of the average number of days per activity times the number of participants and then summed across all activities) increased 32.8 percent from 61.8 billion to 82.0 billion. Average annual days of participation per person increased about 22 percent, from roughly 297 to about 363 total activity days per person per year. (These numbers may seem high, but they represent participation in more than one activity during any given day. So, these averages for "activity days" are sum totals across activities.)

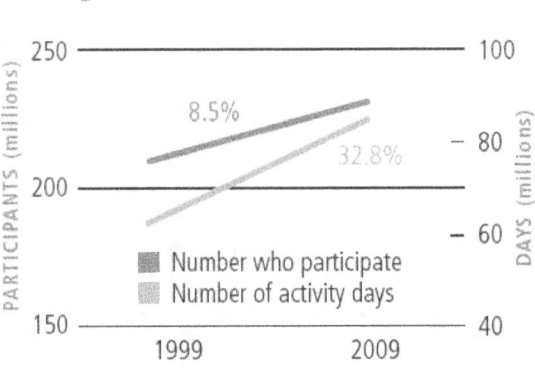

A

3.5%

23.7%

■ Number who participate
■ Number of activity days

PARTICIPANTS (millions): 40, 60, 80, 100
DAYS (billions): 0, 10, 20, 30, 40
1999   2009

B

8.5%

32.8%

■ Number who participate
■ Number of activity days

PARTICIPANTS (millions): 150, 200, 250
DAYS (millions): 40, 60, 80, 100
1999   2009

FIGURE 8

Growth in the number of participants and the number of participation days in 60 outdoor recreation activities in (A) the North and (B) the United States, 1999 to 2009 (Source: U.S. Department of Agriculture Forest Service 2009a).

For the North, both the total number of outdoor recreation participants and total annual activity days grew slower than the national rate. Participants increased by 3.5 percent, from about 90.4 million to 93.5 million, but their total number of annual activity days increased 23.7 percent, from 27.2 billion to 33.6 billion. Average annual activity participation days per person across the full list of activities rose from about 300 per year to 359, a 20 percent increase. Although the number of participants increased only modestly, they engaged in an average of nearly one activity per day over the course of a year (U.S. Department of Agriculture, Forest Service. 2009a). This represents a fairly significant increase in activity level compared to approximately a decade before.

The percentage of the national total number of participants and total population by region is shown for seven activity groups in Table 4. Also listed is the participation rate (percent of the region's population age 16 and older participating) for the four regions.

Table 4—Participation in seven activity groups by individuals aged 16 years and older in four U.S. regions (Source: U.S. Department of Agriculture Forest Service 2009a).

Activity Group (activities that comprise the group)	Region	Region's percent of U.S. participants[a]	Region's percent of U.S. population[a]	Percent of region's population participating
Visiting recreation and historic sites				
(Attending family gatherings, picnicking, visiting the beach, visiting historic or prehistoric sites, and camping)	North	42.0	40.7	82.7
	South	29.7	31.4	78.9
	Rocky Mountains	10.1	10.1	81.9
	Pacific Coast	18.2	17.8	81.4
Viewing/photographing nature				
(View/photograph birds, natural scenery, other wildlife besides birds, and wildflowers, trees, and other plants)	North	40.8	40.7	75.6
	South	30.7	31.4	73.2
	Rocky Mountains	10.5	10.1	78.1
	Pacific Coast	17.9	17.8	75.8
Backcountry activities				
(Backpacking, day hiking, horseback riding on trails, mountain climbing, and visiting a wilderness or primitive area)	North	40.1	40.7	43.1
	South	26.0	31.4	37.4
	Rocky Mountains	13.0	10.1	57.4
	Pacific Coast	20.9	17.8	51.4

Table 4 continued

Activity Group (activities that comprise the group)	Region	Region's percent of U.S. participants[a]	Region's percent of U.S. population[a]	Percent of region's population participating
Motorized activities				
(Motorboating, off-highway-vehicle driving, snowmobiling, using personal watercraft, and waterskiing)	North	40.8	40.7	36.4
	South	31.1	31.4	37.1
	Rocky Mountains	10.7	10.1	39.1
	Pacific Coast	17.4	17.8	35.6
Hunting and fishing				
(Anadromous fishing, coldwater fishing, warmwater fishing, saltwater fishing, big game hunting, small game hunting, and migratory bird hunting)	North	38.6	40.7	32.4
	South	35.5	31.4	38.8
	Rocky Mountains	10.9	10.1	37.1
	Pacific Coast	15.0	17.8	28.8
Non-motorized boating				
(Canoeing, kayaking, rafting, rowing, and sailing)	North	45.6	40.7	23.0
	South	27.5	31.4	18.0
	Rocky Mountains	9.2	10.1	18.7
	Pacific Coast	17.7	17.8	20.4
Snow skiing and boarding				
(Cross country skiing, downhill skiing, and snowboarding)	North	49.6	40.7	14.0
	South	14.5	31.4	5.5
	Rocky Mountains	12.6	10.1	14.7
	Pacific Coast	23.3	17.8	15.1

[a]Percentages sum down to 100 across the four regions of each activity group. May not equal 100.0 exactly due to rounding.

Visiting recreation and historic sites—In general, regional differences are slight with participation in activities at recreation and historic sites slightly greater in the North and slightly lower in the South. The South is the only region whose participation is less than the 81.0 percent national rate, although only about 2 percent less.

Viewing and photographing nature—Participation rates are a few percentage points higher in the Rocky Mountains and Pacific Coast, and a few points lower in the South. The North participation rate of 75.6 percent is identical to the national rate.

Backcountry activities—The percentage of people who participated in backcountry activities is substantially higher in the Rocky Mountains and Pacific Coast than in the Nation as a whole, and is especially higher than in the South. Northern participation in backcountry activities (43.1 percent) is only slightly lower than the national rate of 44.3 percent. Northerners are more likely than people in the South to be backcountry activity participants, but less likely than residents of the West.

Motorized activities—Northern participation is just slightly lower than the national rate (36.9 percent), and lower than all other regions except the Pacific Coast. Participation in motorized activities is slightly higher in the Rocky Mountains than in the other three regions, and the Rocky Mountains is the only region that is more than a few percentage points higher than the national participation rate.

Hunting and fishing—The North lags behind the national rate in hunting and fishing participation, by nearly 2 percent. The South leads all regions in hunting and fishing participation, followed by the Rocky Mountains. Both are higher than the national rate of 34.3 percent. Hunting and fishing participation is somewhat more likely in the North than in the Pacific Coast.

Non-motorized boating activities—Participation in non-motorized boating is highest in the North and Pacific Coast, and lowest in the South. At 23.0 percent participation, the North leads the national rate of 20.8 percent and also has significantly more participation than the South and Rocky Mountains.

Snow skiing and boarding—Snow skiing and snowboarding participation is highest in the Pacific Coast and Rocky Mountains, followed by the North, although the rates for those three regions are separated by just 1.1 percent. Not unexpectedly, participation is by far lowest in the South. Every region but the South exceeds the national participation rate of 11.6 percent. Participation in the South is less than half the national rate. With about 41 percent of the national population, the North has almost half the Nation's skiers and snow boarders.

The popularity of birding and other viewing and learning activities continues throughout the North and the United States, as illustrated by this couple and their grandsons at the Tamarac National Wildlife Refuge in Minnesota. (Photograph courtesy of Lake Country Scenic Byway Association)

THE NORTH'S PARTICIPATION IN NATURE-BASED ACTIVITIES

Tables 5 through 8 summarize the trends in activity participation (number of people and percent of population age 16 and older in the North) in nature-based activities, such as birdwatching or camping, from the mid-1990s to 2009.

Activities that had more than or equal to 30 million people participating are shown in Table 5. Walking for pleasure, attending family gatherings outdoors, gardening or landscaping, viewing/photographing natural scenery, visiting outdoor nature centers or zoos, and picnicking occupied the top six slots, each with over 50 million participants in the North. In the 40-to-50-million participant category were viewing/photographing wildlife (besides birds and fish), viewing/photographing wildflowers/trees/other plants, sightseeing, driving for pleasure, visiting a beach, visiting historic sites, swimming in lakes/ponds/streams, and swimming in an outdoor pool. With a few exceptions—visiting historic sites, picnicking, gardening or landscaping, driving for pleasure, and bicycling, which increased less than 5 percent—all of the most popular activities have shown considerable growth. Activities oriented toward viewing and photographing nature (scenery, flowers/trees/other plants, and wildlife) were among the fastest growing.

Table 5—For activities with greater than 30 million participants annually (2005 to 2009), trends in the number and percentage of people in the North age 16 years and older participating in nature-based activities from 1994 to 2009 (Source: U.S. Department of Agriculture Forest Service 2009a).

Activity	1994 to 1995[a]	1999 to 2001[b]	2005 to 2009[c]		1999 to 2009
	-----Number of participants----- (millions)		Number of participants (millions)	Portion of Population (percent)	Change (percent)
Walking for pleasure	62.9	78.1	82.5	84.6	5.6
Attending family gatherings	58.5	68.2	73.0	74.9	7.1
Gardening or landscaping	—	63.3	64.9	66.6	2.5
Viewing/photographing natural scenery	—	55.4	61.9	63.6	11.8
Visiting an outdoor nature center/zoo	50.2	53.1	55.9	57.3	5.3
Picnicking	52.1	52.6	53.2	54.6	1.0
Viewing/photographing wildlife (other than birds and fish)	29.1	41.2	49.7	51.0	20.5
Viewing/photographing flowers/trees/other plants	—	40.5	49.6	50.9	22.6
Sightseeing	52.6	47.2	49.5	50.8	5.0
Driving for pleasure	—	47.3	49.0	50.3	3.6
Visiting beaches	58.0	38.2	44.1	45.2	15.3
Visiting historic sites	41.1	43.4	43.3	44.4	-0.1
Swimming in lakes/ponds/streams	41.7	39.4	42.7	43.8	8.4
Swimming in outdoor pools	44.9	37.6	41.6	42.7	10.5
Bicycling	36.7	37.1	38.6	39.6	4.1
Viewing or photographing birds	25.5	31.6	37.3	38.2	17.8
Gathering mushrooms/berries	—	27.9	35.0	36.0	25.7
Visiting farm or agricultural settings	—	27.3	34.8	35.7	27.5
Day hiking	22.5	27.7	31.9	32.7	15.1
Visiting wilderness areas	—	27.5	30.5	31.3	10.7

— = Participation in this activity was not asked during this survey period.

[a] Based on regional population of 89.64 million people age 16 years and older (Woods and Poole Economics, Inc. 2009).

[b] Based on regional population of 92.43 million people age 16 years and older (U.S. Department of Commerce, Bureau of the Census 2009a).

[c] Based on regional population of 97.44 million people age 16 years and older (U.S. Department of Commerce, Bureau of the Census 2009a).

Twelve activities had 10 to 30 million participants (Table 6). Viewing or photographing fish, warm water fishing, motor boating, visiting a waterside (besides a beach), sledding, and developed camping all had more than 20 million participants. Four activities—developed camping, mountain biking, primitive camping, and participating in boat tours or excursions—showed a decrease in numbers of participants during the decade. Fastest growing for this period were off-highway-vehicle driving, warm water fishing, and viewing or photographing fish.

Table 6—For activities with 10 to 30 million participants (2005 to 2009), trends in the number and percentage of people in the North age 16 years and older participating in nature-based activities from 1994 to 2009 (Source: U.S. Department of Agriculture Forest Service 2009a).

Activity	1994 to 1995[a]	1999 to 2001[b]	2005 to 2009[c]	1999 to 2009
	-----Number of participants----- (millions)		Number of participants (millions) / Portion of Population (percent)	Change (percent)
Viewing/photographing fish	11.6	21.7	24.6 / 25.2	13.1
Warmwater fishing	22.9	20.4	23.9 / 24.5	17.3
Motorboating	27.1	22.5	23.5 / 24.1	4.7
Visiting watersides (besides beaches)	—	22.6	23.0 / 23.6	1.9
Sledding	17.7	19.8	20.7 / 21.3	4.5
Developed camping	19.6	22.4	20.1 / 20.6	-10.4
Mountain biking	—	21.2	19.8 / 20.3	-6.4
Participating in boat tours or excursions	—	19.1	18.7 / 19.2	-1.9
Visiting prehistoric sites	14.9	17.6	18.1 / 18.6	3.0
Driving off-road	14.0	13.8	17.2 / 17.6	24.8
Canoeing	9.8	11.1	12.0 / 12.3	8.2
Primitive camping	11.8	11.9	11.6 / 11.9	-2.5

— = Participation in this activity was not asked during this survey period.

[a] Based on regional population of 89.64 million people age 16 years and older (Woods and Poole Economics. Inc. 2009).

[b] Based on regional population of 92.43 million people age 16 years and older (U.S. Department of Commerce, Bureau of the Census 2009a).

[c] Based on regional population of 97.44 million people age 16 years and older (U.S. Department of Commerce, Bureau of the Census 2009a).

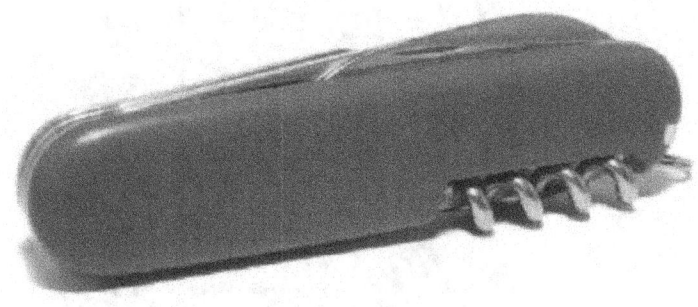

Among the 23 activities with 3 to 10 million participants (Table 7), big game hunting, backpacking, ice skating outdoors, saltwater fishing, and waterskiing were at the top of the list. Seven of the activities posted double-digit percentage growth since 1999; eight activities grew from 0 to 10 percent; and eight activities decreased in number of participants. The fastest growing activities were kayaking (which grew at more than twice the rate of any other activity in this category), snowboarding, and waterskiing. Cross-country skiing, downhill skiing, and rafting posted the largest percent decreases.

Six activities had fewer than 3 million participants (Table 8). At the top of the list, with 2 or more million participants, were orienteering (which grew nearly 91 percent since 1999) and snowshoeing (which decreased more than 17 percent). Given their low participation rates, these activities primarily represent niche markets that appeal to small population segments. Many require substantial investments in time, equipment, and skill.

The participation data shown in Tables 5 through 8 in part may be reflecting the rapid rise in gasoline prices from 2007 to 2008 and the recession that began in 2007. Viewed overall, however, it is clear that what people in the North choose as activities is changing over time. Some of the activities that dominated a generation or two ago no longer dominate with the emergence of underlying changes in society, generations, lifestyles, information, and technology (Cordell 2008).

A timely topic that has captured the attention of many conservation leaders and other interested supporters throughout the Nation is the relationship that America's youth has with natural resources. In particular, many observers have expressed concern over what they see as a growing "disconnect" between children and the outdoors, asserting that children in America are spending increasingly less time outdoors. The following section presents results of a study of their time outdoors that was conducted from 2007 to 2009.

CHILDREN AND THE OUTDOORS

Better understanding of outdoor time and activities among children provides some very important insights into the future. To address this need for better understanding, data from the National Kids Survey were analyzed to estimate the portion of each day that 6-to-19-year-olds spent outdoors during the week preceding their interviews (Cordell 2012). This survey is the only national data source of time and activities by young people outdoors.

Table 7— For activities with 3 to 10 million participants (2005 to 2009), trends in the number and percentage of people in the North age 16 years and older participating in nature-based activities from 1994 to 2009 (Source: U.S. Department of Agriculture Forest Service 2009a).

Activity	1994 to 1995[a]	1999 to 2001[b]	2005 to 2009[c]		1999 to 2009
	-----Number of participants----- (millions)		Number of participants (millions)	Portion of Population (percent)	Change (percent)
Big game hunting	8.6	7.3	8.5	8.7	17.1
Backpacking	6.5	8.5	8.3	8.5	-1.6
Ice skating	10.5	9.1	8.2	8.4	-9.7
Saltwater fishing	8.1	7.9	8.0	8.2	2.0
Waterskiing	9.3	5.9	7.6	7.8	29.2
Horseback riding	7.9	7.1	7.6	7.8	6.1
Use personal watercraft	4.5	7.1	7.4	7.6	3.8
Downhill skiing	11.0	8.7	7.3	7.5	-15.2
Rafting	8.4	8.1	7.0	7.2	-13.2
Snowmobiling	6.5	7.1	6.9	7.1	-2.7
Kayaking	1.4	3.6	6.8	7.0	89.3
Small game hunting	7.5	5.7	6.6	6.8	15.4
Snorkeling[d]	6.4	5.6	5.8	5.9	3.9
Horseback riding on trails	6.1	5.8	5.8	5.9	0.1
Snowboarding	3.3	4.1	5.6	5.8	35.9
Rowing	6.4	4.8	4.9	5.0	1.4
Sailing	5.8	5.5	4.9	5.0	-11.6
Mountain climbing	3.0	4.6	4.1	4.2	-11.6
Caving	3.9	3.1	4.0	4.1	30.0
Rock climbing	2.9	3.5	3.9	4.0	10.0
Cross country skiing	5.8	4.8	3.9	4.0	-20.6
Ice fishing	3.7	3.5	3.8	3.9	9.2
Anadromous fishing	5.0	3.4	3.6	3.7	6.2

[a]Based on regional population of 89.6 million people age 16 years and older (Woods and Poole Economics, Inc. 2009).

[b]Based on regional population of 92.4 million people age 16 years and older (U.S. Department of Commerce, Bureau of the Census 2009a).

[c]Based on regional population of 97.4 million people age 16 years and older (U.S. Department of Commerce, Bureau of the Census 2009a).

[d]Scuba diving was included in the snorkeling activity in this survey period.

Table 8—For activities with less than 3 million participants (2005 to 2009), trends in the number and percentage of people in the North age 16 years and older participating in nature-based activities from 1994 to 2009 (Source: U.S. Department of Agriculture Forest Service 2009a).

Activity	1994 to 1995[a]	1999 to 2001[b]	2005 to 2009[c]		1999 to 2009
	-----Number of participants----- (millions)		Number of participants (millions)	Portion of Population (percent)	Change (percent)
Orienteering	2.1	1.3	2.4	2.5	90.6
Snowshoeing	—[d]	2.7	2.3	2.3	-17.1
Migratory bird hunting	2.0	1.6	1.8	1.8	12.9
Scuba diving	—[e]	1.4	1.5	1.5	6.7
Surfing	0.8	0.8	1.1	1.1	43.4
Windsurfing	1.2	0.7	0.8	0.8	3.7

— = *Missing data.*

[a]*Based on regional population of 89.64 million people age 16 years and older (Woods and Poole Economics, Inc. 2009).*

[b]*Based on regional population of 92.43 million people age 16 years and older (U.S. Department of Commerce, Bureau of the Census 2009a).*

[c]*Based on regional population of 97.44 million people age 16 years and older (U.S. Department of Commerce, Bureau of the Census 2009a).*

[d]*Participation in this activity was not asked during this survey period.*

[e]*Scuba diving was included as part of snorkeling in 1994 to 1995.*

Estimates from the kids survey included outdoor time during a typical weekday and typical weekend day (Table 9). As well, current estimates of time outdoors per day are compared to the previous year (Table 10). Nationally, about 62 percent reported spending two or more hours outdoors per day on a typical weekday and 77 percent on typical weekend days, compared to 58 percent on weekdays and 74 percent on weekends in the North (Table 9). Just under half of youths nationwide spent 4 or more hours outdoors on a typical weekend day, compared to 43 percent of North region youths. Less than 5 percent spent no time outdoors on either weekdays or weekend days regardless of where the youth lived. As one might expect, school and other activities that are not necessarily recreation likely compose a significant amount of youth time outdoors during weekdays.

Table 9—For 6- to 19-year-olds in the United States and Northern States, time spent outdoors on typical weekdays and weekend days.

Amount of time	Respondents (percent)	
	On weekdays	On weekend days
United States		
None	2.3	3.9
<1/2 hour a day	4.3	2.2
About 1/2 hour a day	8.1	3.5
About 1 hour	23.1	13.3
2-3 hours	33.8	27.3
≥4 hours	28.5	49.8
Northern States		
None	3.3	4.5
<1/2 hour a day	4.0	1.8
About 1/2 hour a day	9.2	3.8
About 1 hour	25.5	15.7
2-3 hours	32.2	31.1
≥4 hours	25.9	43.1

Note: Percent may not sum down within the United States and North to 100.0 exactly due to rounding.

Source: Larson et al. (2011).

Table 10—For 6- to 19-year-olds in the United States and Northern States, amount of time spent outdoors compared to the same time last year.

Sample	Less time	About the same	More time
		(percent)	
United States	15.5	44.9	39.6
Northern States	17.0	49.0	34.0

Note: Percent may not sum across within the United States and North to 100.0 exactly due to rounding.

Source: Larson et al. 2011.

Next examined were percentages who indicated spending less, the same or more time outdoors at the time of the interview relative to a year ago. Across the entire sample, both boys and girls, only about 16 percent reported spending less time, 45 percent reported spending the same, and 40 percent estimated spending more time outdoors this year than last (Table 10). In the North, respondents were slightly more likely to report spending less time outdoors than they did a year ago (17 percent), more likely to say they spent about the same amount of time outdoors (49 percent), and less likely to say they spent more time outdoors (34 percent).

Table 11 compares outdoor activity participation rates (percentages) between male and female respondents in the North and the Nation. Playing outdoors or "hanging out" during the previous week was the most common activity, with about 84 percent participating.

Male participation in this unstructured free play was higher both nationwide and in the North. The grouping of biking/jogging/walking/skateboarding or similar activities was the next most popular with nearly 80 percent participating both nationally and in the North. For both samples, female participation was slightly higher than male participation. Listening to music or using a screen or other electronic device outdoors was the third most cited outdoor activity with about 51 percent participating. This activity was slightly more popular with girls than with boys. These data indicate that the use of electronic media is not limited to indoor settings. Nationally, playing or practicing team sports was considerably more popular with boys, but less so in the North. By contrast, reading or studying while sitting outdoors was more popular with girls, both nationally and in the North.

Many children and teenagers enjoy spending time outdoors in nature-based recreation as well as in other activities closer to home. Here, children learn how to kayak in the Hiawatha National Forest in Michigan. (Photograph by Anne Okonek)

Table 11—For 6- to 19-year-olds in the United States and Northern States, participation (percent) in outdoor activities during the past week, by gender.

Outdoor activities	United States			Northern States		
	Male	Female	Total	Male	Female	Total
Just playing outdoors or hanging out	87.1	81.8	84.5	87.9	79.4	83.9
Biking/jogging/walking/skateboarding	78.3	81.4	79.7	75.8	82.4	78.8
Listening to music or using other electronic devices	48.2	55.2	51.6	48.5	53.8	51.0
Playing or practicing team sports	59.5	38.8	49.3	54.7	43.8	49.5
Reading or studying while sitting outdoors	38.5	53.5	45.8	36.8	52.8	44.2
Participating in individual sports, (such as tennis, golf)	38.0	35.2	36.6	34.7	38.4	36.5
Attending camps, field trips, outdoor classes	34.1	39.1	36.5	36.1	37.1	36.3
Swimming, diving, snorkeling	30.8	32.1	31.5	32.5	24.4	28.7
Birdwatching and wildlife viewing	28.5	32.3	30.4	30.2	27.4	28.9
Hiking, camping, fishing	30.8	28.2	29.5	36.1	24.9	30.9
Riding motorcycles, all-terrain vehicles, other off-road vehicles	24.2	14.4	19.4	23.7	13.7	19.0
Boating, jet skiing, water skiing	9.1	7.2	8.2	8.4	4.5	6.5
Snow skiing, snowboarding, cross-country skiing	8.6	6.6	7.6	12.2	8.7	10.6
Rowing, kayaking, canoeing, surfing	8.1	6.8	7.5	7.3	7.4	7.4
Participating in other activities	10.3	11.6	10.9	13.8	8.6	11.3

Note: Each activity asked separately; sample sizes vary.

More than a third of respondents participated in other sports such as golf and tennis and in organized nature-based activities such as attending outdoor camps, classes, and field trips. These two activity groups had nearly identical participation rates of 36 percent, both nationally and in the North. Gender differences were slight in both samples. In the North, a number of other nature-based activities (swimming, diving, snorkeling, birdwatching, wildlife viewing, and hiking, camping, fishing) each experienced about 30 percent participation. Boys outpaced girls in the motorized activity of riding off-road vehicles by about 10 percent both nationally and in the North. Hiking, camping, and fishing participation also was higher for males than females in the North.

Table 12 shows participation by age group for the same set of activities in the North and for the United States In both samples, unstructured free play decreased with age; biking/jogging/walking/skateboarding decreased up to age 15 and then rebounded slightly with the oldest age group of 16- to-19-year-olds. Electronic media use outdoors is much less frequent with the youngest age group, but then rises with age until peaking with the 13- to-15-year-age group.

In both the North and the Nation, team sports also peaked with the early teenage group, but participation in reading or studying outdoors was considerably higher for the oldest teens than for the three younger groups. Other, mostly individual sports, ranked higher in the 10- to-12-year-old group and also in the youngest group, relative to the two older ones. This may be indicative of more children beginning these activities at an early age then dropping out to pursue other interests as they get older. Interestingly, activities such as attending outdoor classes and camps was most popular nationwide with the youngest age group, but most popular in the North with the oldest age group. This may be because the northeastern area has a stronger tradition of organized camps and more organized camping facilities than other parts of the country. Participation rates for these activities were fairly consistently in the 33-to-40-percent range regardless of age or location. Birdwatching and wildlife viewing decreased significantly with age in both samples, which may be an indicator of family outings in which teenagers do not participate. Off-road vehicle driving and boating activities increased with age in both samples, although boating participation peaked with early teens nationally and with 10- to-12-year-olds in the North.

Table 12—For 6- to 19-year-olds in the United States and Northern States, participation (percent) in outdoor activities during the past week, by age group.

Outdoor activities	United States				Northern States			
	Age 6 to 9	Age 10 to 12	Age 13 to 15	Age 16 to 19	Age 6 to 9	Age 10 to 12	Age 13 to 15	Age 16 to 19
Just playing outdoors or hanging out	91.5	95.4	82.8	69.8	90.2	93.2	82.9	71.6
Biking/jogging/walking/ skateboarding	85.1	82.8	70.9	78.7	82.1	79.4	74.4	78.5
Listening to music, watching movies, using electronics	33.4	50.0	63.8	63.8	34.7	51.4	59.6	59.1
Playing or practicing team sports	45.1	49.4	56.5	48.6	43.3	51.3	56.2	50.0
Reading or studying while sitting outdoors	42.1	47.0	36.2	56.3	41.2	39.1	37.0	56.9
Participating in individual sports (such as tennis, golf)	41.7	45.0	28.1	31.3	38.2	44.5	31.3	33.1
Attending camps, field trips, outdoor classes	40.6	37.3	33.2	34.0	36.4	35.5	34.5	39.1
Swimming, diving, snorkeling	31.5	32.2	31.5	30.6	27.4	29.3	29.0	29.1
Birdwatching and wildlife viewing	40.9	36.8	23.8	19.3	35.9	38.9	29.8	14.0
Hiking, camping, fishing	34.3	26.2	27.5	28.6	32.2	34.3	29.0	28.6
Riding motorcycles, all-terrain vehicles, other off-road driving	17.8	13.2	22.1	24.1	16.7	18.0	20.4	21.2
Boating, jet skiing, water skiing	6.7	7.3	13.0	9.9	3.4	8.0	6.7	8.7
Snow skiing, snowboarding, cross-country skiing	7.0	8.2	8.9	8.7	10.1	16.7	6.8	10.0
Rowing, kayaking, canoeing, surfing	5.7	8.4	6.2	10.2	4.1	9.9	5.8	10.4
Participating in other activities	9.7	11.3	5.4	10.4	7.8	10.9	16.4	10.8

Note: Each activity asked separately; sample sizes vary.

Source: Larson et al. 2011

Federal land—Nationally, Federal agencies manage nearly 640 million acres, much of which includes vast areas suitable for a variety of outdoor recreation activities. Such areas are as important in the North as they are throughout the country. Other than some national wildlife refuges areas reserved for science and research, dams, and other administrative and operational sites, very little Federal land is closed or has restrictions on public access, but access is sometimes blocked by in-holdings and ownership fragmentation.

Less than 3 percent of Federal land (about 17.9 million acres) is in the North, about 69 percent of which is managed by the Forest Service. More than 92 percent of Federal land is located in the western United States. Even not counting Alaska, which has 36 percent of the national total, Federal land is predominantly western, making up 88 percent of the 49-State total area. The regional distribution of acreage in the three water resources agencies (U.S. Army Corps of Engineers, U.S. Department of the Interior Bureau of Reclamation, and Tennessee Valley Authority), however, is much more evenly distributed between the West and East. Of the total land and water area in these three agencies, nearly half is located in the East, about 12 percent in the North and 37 percent in the South.

Federal acreage changes very little over time. What does change, however, particularly by region, is the amount of Federal land per capita as population grows. In 2008, the 2,105 acres per 1,000 U.S. residents (or about 2.1 acres per person) represented a 5.6 percent decrease from the 2002 level. Decreases were largest in the Rocky Mountains (8.8 percent) and Pacific Coast (7.7 percent), reflecting greater population growth in those regions. The North, with 143.6 Federal acres per 1,000 persons, had the smallest regional decrease (-2.4 percent).

The decrease in per capita Federal acres nationally was even more pronounced when compared to 1995 levels, mirroring the 14 percent population increase (Table 13). The 8.2 percent decrease in Federal acres per capita in the North was the slowest of any region and considerably less than the national rate of change. Nonetheless, pressures for recreation space in the North are likely to increase as population grows, albeit more slowly than in the past.

Wilderness—The North accounts for just 1.5 percent, or about 1.7 million of the 109.5 million acres in the National Wilderness Preservation System. Similar to Federal land in general, the Wilderness land managed by four Federal agencies lies mostly in Western States (96 percent). Alaska, in particular, has more than 52 percent of the total system—largely managed by the U.S. Department of the Interior National Park Service and U.S. Department of the Interior Fish and Wildlife Service.

Table 13—Federal acres per 1,000 people (including Alaska) in 1995 and percentage change from 1995 to 2008, by region; estimated U.S. population was 266.28 million (Woods and Poole Economics, Inc. 2009) for 1995 and 304.06 million (U.S. Department of Commerce, Bureau of the Census 2009a) for 2008 (Sources: U.S. Department of Agriculture Forest Service 1995, 2008; U.S. Department of the Interior National Park Service 1995, 2008; U.S. Department of the Interior Fish and Wildlife Service 1995, 2008; U.S. Department of the Interior Bureau of Reclamation 1993, 2008; U.S. Department of the Interior Bureau of Land Management 1994, 2008; Tennessee Valley Authority 2008; U.S. Army Corps of Engineers 2006).

Agency	North		South		Rocky Mountains		Pacific Coast		United States	
	Acres 1995[a]	Percent Change 2008	Acres 1995[a]	Percent Change 2008	Acres 1995[a]	Percent Change 2008	Acres 1995[a]	Percent Change 2008	Acres 1995[a]	Percent Change 2008
Forest Service	101.9	-3.4	151.7	-14.6	4,600.3	-22.3	1,581.1	-12.7	719.6	-11.9
National Park Service	11.0	-1.8	58.3	-13.4	482.5	-17.5	1,447.3	-13.8	292.0	-11.2
Fish and Wildlife Service	10.3	34.0	44.8	-5.4	330.6	7.6	1,855.6	-13.7	339.7	-8.5
Bureau of Reclamation	0.0	0.0	2.3	-17.4	251.4	-21.8	20.3	-14.3	24.5	-12.7
Bureau of Land Management	3.3	-100.0	9.4	-95.7	6,629.1	-22.5	2,898.7	-22.4	1,005.1	-17.1
Tennessee Valley Authority	0.0	0.0	2.9	-17.2	0.0	0.0	0.0	0.0	0.9	-11.1
Army Corps of Engineers	24.8	-16.9	66.2	4.4	113.8	11.9	12.8	-13.3	43.4	4.1
All agencies	156.4	-8.2	350.2	-15.4	12,422.9	-21.2	7,911.8	-17.8	2,448.6	-14.0

[a] Resource data years for earlier period vary by agency; expressed as 1995 because 1995 population estimates were used in per capita measures.

Without the Alaska acres, the North's share of wilderness rises only to 3.2 percent of the Nation's total.

Since 1995, wilderness system area has grown about 6 percent, but population increases have reduced the national per capita acres by 3 percent (Table 14). In the South, the decrease was nearly 16 percent, followed by 10 percent for Oregon, California, and Washington on the Pacific Coast, and 8 percent for the Rocky Mountains. Only the North experienced an increase since 1995, although at 1.5 percent, just slightly. In the 49 States, per capita wilderness acres decreased across all agencies, except for the U.S. Department of the Interior Bureau of Land Management. All of the wilderness system acreage added in the North region is managed by the National Park Service.

Table 14—Federal acres in the National Wilderness Preservation System (excluding Alaska) per 1,000 people in 1995[a] and percentage change from 1995 to 2009[b], by region; estimated U.S. population was 265.67 million, excluding Alaska (Woods and Poole Economics, Inc. 2009) for 1995 and 303.37 million, excluding Alaska (U.S. Department of Commerce, Bureau of the Census 2009a) for 2008 (Source: Wilderness.net 2009).

Agency	North		South		Rocky Mountains		Pacific Coast		United States	
	Acres 1995	Percent Change 2009	Acres 1995	Percent Change 2009	Acres 1995	Percent Change 2009	Acres 1995	Percent Change 2009	Acres 1995	Percent Change 2009
Bureau of Land Management[a]	0.0	0.0	0.0	0.0	74.8	121.4	89.5	-3.5	20.0	44.0
Fish and Wildlife Service[a]	0.5	0.0	5.5	-16.4	67.3	-21.7	0.3	-33.3	7.6	-11.8
Forest Service[b]	11.5	0.0	8.3	-12.0	823.1	-20.5	237.8	-9.1	111.5	-9.5
National Park Service[a]	1.1	27.3	17.5	-17.1	36.0	34.2	200.9	-13.8	39.0	-6.9
U.S. Total	13.2	1.5	31.3	-15.7	1,001.2	-8.0	505.2	-9.8	176.9	-3.0

[a]U.S. Department of the Interior

[b]U.S. Department of Agriculture

Protected rivers and trails—Two Federal systems play a key role in resource protection and outdoor recreation. They are the National Wild and Scenic Rivers System and the National Recreation Trails System, both established by Congress in 1968. The currently more than 12,500 miles of wild and scenic rivers in the United States represent an 11 percent increase since 2000 (Table 15); 3,000 miles are in the East and the remaining 76 percent are in the West. These rivers—which are classified as wild, scenic, or recreational—range from the most primitive and undeveloped (wild) to the most accessible and (perhaps) impounded in the past (recreational). The North has nearly 2,200 miles (about 17 percent of the national total), an increase of 6 percent since 2000. Most of the 125 miles added in the North are in the scenic and recreational classifications, with only 2 miles in the wild classification.

The National Trails System consists of three categories of nationally significant trails: National Scenic Trails, National Historic Trails, and National Recreation Trails. Similar to the federally designated rivers, national trails protect linear land resources that are judged to have significant value for the entire country.

The scenic and historic category typically consists of long overland trails that are remote from population centers, compared to recreation trails, which tend to be located near or within urban areas. As of 2009 the United States had more than 1,000 national recreation trails totaling more than 20,000 miles (Table 16); of these, 53 percent of the trails and nearly 69 percent of the mileage are located in the populous East. The North, which had more than 7,300 miles and 36 percent of the system, has added more trails than any other region and more miles of trails (3,200) than any other region except the South, which saw 84 percent growth in trail miles since 2004.

Recreation facilities—The Recreation Information Database, an interagency effort coordinated by the U.S. Department of the Interior, is a public data portal on Federal recreation sites and facilities throughout the country. Table 17 shows that the Nation's estimated 9,075 Federal facilities translate into just under 30 facilities per million people (or about 1 per 33,500). With just 9.5 facilities per million people overall (or about 1 per 105,000), the North lags behind the western regions by a wide margin. The combination of much more Federal property and much less population in the West is a primary reason for this disparity. The North also lags behind the South, which has more camping and boating facilities but is about even in other facilities. The Rocky Mountains has more than 10 times the number of available Federal facilities per capita than both the South and the North and has nearly twice as many as the Pacific Coast. Camping facilities dominate in the listing of facilities being offered at nearly 96 percent of areas nationwide.

Table 15—Miles of river in the National Wild and Scenic River System by classification and region, 2000 and 2009, with percentage change (includes AK and HI) (Source: Interagency Wild and Scenic Rivers Council 2009).

	Wild rivers			Scenic rivers			Recreational rivers			Total		
	2000 (miles)	2009 (miles)	Percent Change	2000 (miles)	2009 (miles)	Percent Change	2000 (miles)	2009 (miles)	Percent Change	2000 (miles)	2009 (miles)	Percent Change
North	172	174	1.5	935	1,014	8.5	964	1,007	4.4	2,070	2,195	6.0
South	187	284	51.8	318	414	30.2	112	112	0.0	617	810	31.3
Rocky Mountains	710	1,328	87.1	288	380	31.9	532	587	10.5	1,530	2,295	50.0
Pacific Coast	4,280	4,370	2.1	911	936	2.7	1,886	1,946	3.2	7,077	7,252	2.5
U.S. total	5,349	6,156	15.1	2,452	2,743	11.9	3,493	3,652	4.6	11,294	12,552	11.1

Table 16—Number and miles of National Recreation Trails by region, 2004 and 2009, with percentage change (Source: American Trails 2010) (includes AK and HI).

| Region | National Recreation Trails | | | | | |
| | Number | | Percent Change | Miles | | Percent Change |
	2004	2009		2004	2009	
North	226	312	38.1	4,119	7,319	77.7
South	220	264	20.0	3,578	6,577	83.8
Rocky Mountains	254	292	15.0	2,969	3,380	13.8
Pacific Coast	198	209	5.6	2,622	2,944	12.3
U.S. total	898	1,077	19.9	13,288	20,220	52.2

NON-FEDERAL RECREATIONAL RESOURCES

State parks—Each of the 50 States has a State park system, which is usually a division or agency within the department of natural resources or conservation. These resources are usually closer to population centers and more developed than their Federal counterparts. Although most State park systems manage a significant number of backcountry acres, remote holdings are not nearly as common as they are in Federal systems. State parks have been called "intermediate" resources because they represent a middle ground between the sometimes vast and distant Federal lands and the usually much smaller and more highly developed parks managed by local governments (Clawson and Knetsch 1966).

State systems predominantly feature State parks, but they also include facilities classified as recreation areas, natural areas, historic sites, environmental education and science areas, State forests, and wildlife and fish management areas. Although these other types of protected areas may exist separately from State park systems, they are usually still housed within natural resource departments, as are most—but not all— wildlife and fish areas and State forests.

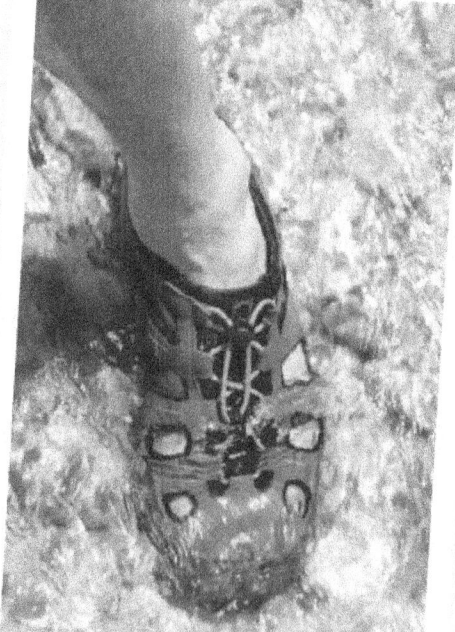

Table 17—Federal recreation facilities provided or activities permitted per million people by region, 2009; based U.S. population estimate of 304.06 million (U.S. Department of Commerce, Bureau of the Census 2009a) in 2008 (includes AK and HI) (Source: U.S. Department of the Interior 2009).

Activity or facility	North	South	Rocky Mountains	Pacific Coast	United States
			Number available (per million people)[a]		
Camping	8.3	11.2	121.3	63.8	28.6
Hiking	1.5	1.8	65.6	19.9	10.4
Fishing	1.3	2.4	64.0	18.3	10.2
Boating	1.9	4.3	22.7	10.2	5.9
Picnicking	0.1	0.1	43.6	9.3	5.6
Recreational vehicle camping	0.0	0.0	38.0	11.7	5.4
Biking	0.4	0.4	32.4	5.7	4.2
Horseback riding	0.1	0.4	27.5	4.7	3.5
Hunting	0.4	0.8	24.8	4.2	3.4
Wildlife viewing	0.1	0.1	20.1	7.5	3.1
Auto touring	0.0	0.0	13.4	2.4	1.6
Water sports	0.0	0.0	6.4	3.9	1.2
Interpretive programs	0.8	0.7	4.7	1.3	1.2
Visitor centers	0.9	0.8	4.0	1.1	1.2
Riding off highway vehicles	0.0	0.0	9.3	1.2	1.0
Wildernesses	0.0	0.0	6.0	2.3	0.9
Winter sports	0.0	0.0	6.3	0.8	0.7
Swimming sites	0.0	0.0	2.2	2.8	0.6
Historic and cultural sites	0.2	0.0	4.0	0.5	0.5
Fish hatcheries	0.1	0.2	0.7	0.3	0.2
Day use areas	0.0	0.0	1.4	0.4	0.2
Climbing	0.0	0.0	1.5	0.2	0.2
All activities and facilities	9.5	12.1	124.2	65.2	29.8

Note: Activities shown as 0.0 reflect <0.05 per million people.

State park systems are usually accessible to the general public as is evidenced by their distribution across U.S. counties (Fig. 9), the majority of which have some acreage of State park system lands. Numerous State park system areas are evident throughout much of the northeastern and midwestern areas, Florida, and along the Pacific Coast. Although there are many fewer state parks in the West, they tend to be large. And although many of the largest properties are found in the West, State park system resources are also numerous throughout the East and particularly on the northern seaboard. With the exception of some parts of the Great Plains and a few other scattered regions across the country, it is rare to travel across more than just a few counties without encountering State park system lands.

Because State parks typically provide a diversity of recreation opportunities, many of the activities that people enjoy on Federal lands can also be enjoyed on the State park system lands. In the North, a State park is located within an hour's drive regardless of where one is located; the few exceptions to this rule are mostly in remote areas of northern Maine and upstate New York.

FIGURE 9

Location and status of State park system units and acres by county in the contiguous United States, 2009 (Source: U.S. Department of Agriculture Forest Service 2009b).

<787 acres
787 to 3,327 acres
3,327 to 12,045 acres
>12,045 acres
● Park closed
● Park open

The Adirondack and Catskill Forest Preserves in New York, although not technically classified as State parks, encompass nearly 3 million acres of State-owned public land and provide numerous outdoor recreation opportunities. Furthermore, Maine, New Hampshire, Vermont, and New York all have a longstanding tradition of public access to private forest lands, particularly on parcels of 1,000 acres or more (Daigle et al. 2012).

The National Association of State Park Directors reported in their 2009 Annual Information Exchange that more than 13.9 million acres exist in State park systems, an increase of about 3 percent in acres per 1,000 people since 1995 (Table 18). Northern States reported about 5.2 million acres (37 percent of the national total or nearly 49 percent if Alaska's large State parks are removed from the Pacific Coast total). State park acreage per capita fell 2 percent from 1995 to 2008 in the North. However, State recreation area acreage per capita increased 50 percent in the North during this period. The North growth in per capita acres across all categories of areas under State park system management was more than 33 percent, about 10 times that of the Nation. It should be noted, however, that most of the North's increase was likely due to the reclassification of other State properties into the State park system's jurisdiction. This was particularly the case in New York State, which included data on the

Most State parks are located within easy access of population centers but still have many wildland characteristics, such as the Devils Lake State Park in Wisconsin. (Photograph by Greg Walther)

Forest Preserves and other properties managed by the Department of Environmental Conservation in the Annual Information Exchange report.

State park systems have faced difficult budgetary pressures since the onset of the 2007 recession. There have been occasional closures of some parks (for example, four in Arizona in 2010), transfers of some to other government and quasi-government entities, and reduced hours, services, and staffing (Table 19). The two affected States located in the North were Massachusetts and Michigan.

Table 18—State park system area per 1,000 people in 1995 and percentage change from 1995 to 2008, by region; estimated U.S. population was 266.28 million (Woods and Poole Economics, Inc. 2009) for 1995 and 304.06 million (U.S. Department of Commerce, Bureau of the Census 2009a) for 2008 (includes AK and HI) (Source: National Association of State Park Directors 1996, 2009).

Type	North		South		Rocky Mountains		Pacific Coast		United States	
	Acres 1995	Percent Change 2008	Acres 1995	Percent Change 2008	Acres 1995	Percent Change 2008	Acres 1995	Percent Change 2008	Acres 1995	Percent Change 2008
State parks	18.0	-2.3	10.1	40.2	37.0	-12.8	95.3	-8.1	29.4	-1.1
Recreation areas	1.5	49.7	1.3	-28.8	8.9	-22.9	18.1	-28.1	4.7	-15.0
Historic sites	0.1	123.1	0.3	-8.8	1.2	-59.8	0.4	51.2	0.3	12.1
Natural areas[a]	0.9	77.6	0.1	9066.7[b]	0.3	2907.4[b]	0.0	.	0.4	804.9
Other areas[c]	9.4	111.6	0.6	-7.9	14.4	-87.1	1.2	7.5	5.7	52.5
All areas	31.2	33.2	19.7	8.8	70.5	-29.7	117.4	-10.1	44.4	3.2

[a]*Includes environmental education sites and areas classified as scientific sites. Large changes are likely to be the result of system reclassifications and not additions.*

[b]*Very large percentage change is primarily the result of system reclassifications and not additions.*

[c]*Includes forests, fish and wildlife areas, and other miscellaneous State park system sites.*

State facilities—Table 20 shows the eight major types of facilities provided by State park systems and trends in these facilities since 1995. Of these, campsites are by far the most numerous. Nationally, access to improved (or developed) campsites, cabins, golf courses, and marinas held steady since 1995, but fell by about 12 percent for primitive campsites. In the North, the decrease in primitive campsites per capita was particularly sharp, falling by about 31 percent. Improved campsites, however, increased by 15 percent; when combined with losses in the South and Pacific Coast, the result was little to no net change nationwide.

The drop in the number of swimming pools per capita at Northern State parks was in the same direction as the national trend. The region also experienced a reduction in the number of stables per capita, but the base year number in 1995 was already relatively small.

Local governments—The 2007 Census of Governments tallied 8,852 local governments that provide recreation and park services, with more than 48 percent of these (4,273 units) in the North. On a proportional basis (per million people) the North experienced about 14 percent growth since 1997, just slightly higher than the national rate of 13 percent (Table 21).

Table 19—State park systems affected by closure or reduction in services as of 2009 (Source: U.S. Department of Agriculture Forest Service 2009b).

State	Total facilities	Number of closures	Reduction in services
Alabama	23	None	One park transferred to county government.
Arizona	28	Two parks and two historic sites	Reduced hours for two State parks and five historic parks.
Georgia	63	None	One park changed to outdoor recreation area; reduced. hours for six historic parks/sites; and three historic sites now operated by the counties within which they reside.
Hawaii	50	None	One park transferred to a development corporation.
Massachusetts	136	Two State forests	Staffing eliminated for two areas.
Michigan	93	None	Reduced summer hours for one site.

Table 20—State park system area per 1,000 people in 1995 and percentage change from 1995 to 2008, by region; estimated U.S. population was 266.28 million (Woods and Poole Economics, Inc. 2009) for 1995 and 304.06 million (U.S. Department of Commerce, Bureau of the Census 2009a) for 2008 (includes AK and HI) (Source: National Association of State Park Directors 1996, 2009).

Facility	North		South		Rocky Mountains		Pacific Coast		United States	
	Acres 1995	Percent Change 2008	Acres 1995	Percent Change 2008	Acres 1995	Percent Change 2008	Acres 1995	Percent Change 2008	Acres 1995	Percent Change 2008
Improved campsites	608.1	15.0	361.1	-2.4	837.2	4.7	514.8	-40.4	533.2	0.3
Primitive campsites	144.4	-31.3	60.6	28.7	855.1	-5.4	215.0	-30.5	186.9	-11.7
Cabins	23.3	11.7	30.1	-11.2	17.3	50.4	9.7	29.0	22.8	5.5
Golf courses	0.4	19.5	0.6	-3.2	0.2	38.9	0.1	-42.9	0.4	4.8
Golf holes	6.4	28.2	9.8	3.3	2.5	108.9	1.7	-46.2	6.4	15.1
Marinas	0.8	29.8	1.0	-22.9	2.5	-10.7	0.3	0.0	0.9	3.3
Swimming pools	1.4	-8.1	1.5	-19.9	0.4	8.1	0.1	100.0	1.1	-12.6
Stables	0.3	-10.0	0.3	92.6	0.6	-40.0	0.1	-77.8	0.3	14.3

Table 21—Number of local government parks and recreation departments per million people in 1997 and 2007, and percentage change from 1997 to 2007; estimated U.S. population was 272.65 million (Woods and Poole Economics, Inc. 2009) for 1997 and 301.29 million (U.S. Department of Commerce, Bureau of the Census 2009a) for 2009 (includes AK and HI) (Source: U.S. Department of Commerce, Bureau of the Census 2007a).

	North			South			Rocky Mountains			Pacific Coast			United States		
	1997	2007	Percent Change	1997	2007	Percent Change	1997	2007	Percent Change	1997	2007	Percent Change	1997	2007	Percent Change
County	3.5	3.5	0.3	5.4	5.7	6.2	5.8	5.1	-12.6	2.3	2.2	-5.6	4.1	4.2	1.7
Municipal	15.0	18.4	22.7	15.5	18.8	20.7	21.0	29.4	40.3	12.9	14.0	8.0	15.3	18.8	22.6
Town or Township	8.5	9.4	11.0	0.0	0.0	0.0	0.0	0.2	0.0	0.0	0.0	0.0	3.7	3.9	5.1
Special District	3.4	3.2	-5.6	0.5	0.7	53.2	7.6	4.8	-37.1	3.8	3.4	-11.3	2.9	2.5	-11.5
All units	30.3	34.5	13.6	21.4	25.2	17.7	34.4	39.5	14.8	19.1	19.5	2.5	26.0	29.4	13.0

Municipal recreation departments grew much faster (23 percent) than county departments and at about twice the rate of township agencies. Special recreation and park districts were the only type of local government jurisdiction that experienced reductions since 1997. The number of special districts and county recreation and park departments was much smaller than the number of municipal or township departments, which averaged 3 million residents. (Special districts are authorized by State legislatures to perform a single function or a limited number of functions including but not limited to water and sewage, irrigation, fire control, primary/secondary/technical education, and hospital administration. Park and recreation services are included among these functions, sometimes as a sole purpose, and at other times as one of many purposes, such as in conservancy.)

Two examples of northern local government agencies that are specifically oriented toward natural resources conservation and recreation are the Wisconsin County Forests and the Illinois County Forest Preserve special districts. The Wisconsin county forests protect more than 2.3 million acres of public forest land in 29 counties and offer a variety of nature-based recreation opportunities. Likewise, in Illinois, the Forest Preserve Districts protect designated lands as "forest preserves" for conservation, education, and "compatible" outdoor recreation experiences. One such example is the Forest Preserve District of Cook County, which manages 68,000 acres of forest, prairie, and wetlands in and around Chicago.

Private providers—Among the nine outdoor recreation business categories tracked by the Census Bureau's County Business Patterns, five showed a decrease in the number of establishments per million people from 1998 to 2007 (Table 22). In the North, amusement/theme parks, recreational/vacation camps, golf courses, and marinas all posted decreases, with amusement and theme parks falling by almost half. Private-sector zoos/botanical gardens, nature parks, and historical sites—all in the viewing/learning/photography group of activities—posted the largest gains. Recreational vehicle parks and campgrounds (4.1 percent growth) was the only category that exceeded the national growth rate (1.4 percent).

Table 22—Number of selected private recreation business establishments per million people in 1998 and percentage change from 1998 to 2007; estimated U.S. population was 272.65 million (Woods and Poole Economics, Inc. 2009) for 1998 and 301.29 million (U.S. Department of Commerce, Bureau of the Census 2009a) for 2007 (includes AK and HI) (Source: U.S. Department of Commerce, Bureau of the Census 2007b).

Recreation business entity	North		South		Rocky Mountains		Pacific Coast		United States	
	1998	Percent Change 2007	1998	Percent Change 2007	1998	Percent Change 2007	1998	Percent Change 2007	1998	Percent Change 2007
Golf courses and country clubs	49.8	-4.3	40.1	-11.7	47.1	-6.0	26.0	-8.8	42.6	-7.7
Recreational vehicle parks and campgrounds	13.3	4.1	11.4	0.4	26.9	-1.3	17.3	-3.1	14.5	1.4
Marinas	17.7	-3.5	16.5	-18.6	7.5	-24.9	10.6	-12.3	15.3	-11.5
Recreational and vacation camps (not campgrounds)	14.0	-18.1	8.5	-20.7	22.5	-28.4	11.3	-12.2	12.5	-19.6
Historical sites	4.5	6.1	2.3	23.9	3.8	-15.2	1.8	3.4	3.3	6.7
Nature parks and similar institutions	1.9	31.7	1.5	35.6	2.9	20.7	1.3	118.5	1.7	42.5
Amusement and theme parks	3.7	-47.8	3.6	-36.8	2.9	-16.6	2.4	-12.9	3.4	-37.7
Zoos and botanical gardens	1.4	33.8	1.3	44.8	1.7	15.5	1.5	49.3	1.4	37.8
Skiing facilities	1.7	0.6	0.4	-40.5	4.4	-7.7	1.5	-17.6	1.5	-8.3

Federal and State parkland—Figure 10 shows county-level availability of Federal and State parkland within a 75-mile radius, the distance considered to be the maximum distance of most day trips, with no overnight stay necessary. Whereas some counties have no Federal or State land within their boundaries, all have some public acreage if acreages in surrounding counties are considered. The large majority of counties in the North have fewer than 1,461 acres of public land per 1,000 persons, with numerous counties having less than 70 acres per 1,000 people. These least abundant areas are concentrated around the northeastern metropolises stretching from Maryland to Boston; in western New York; throughout much of Ohio, Indiana, and southern Michigan; in the urban region extending from greater Chicago to Milwaukee; and from the area near metropolitan Kansas City up through western Iowa to the Twin Cities. The relatively more abundant categories of 1,461 to 18,310 acres per 1,000 people are concentrated in a large region extending across northern Minnesota and Wisconsin to the Upper Peninsula of Michigan and the northernmost counties of the Lower Peninsula; smaller pockets also exist

FIGURE 10

Federal and State parkland area within a 75-mile recreation day trip of each U.S. county 2008 (Sources: U.S. Department of Agriculture Forest Service 2008; U.S. Department of Interior National Park Service 2008; U.S. Department of Interior Bureau of Land Management 2008a; Tennessee Valley Authority 2008; U.S. Army Corps of Engineers 2006; National Association of State Park Directors 2009).

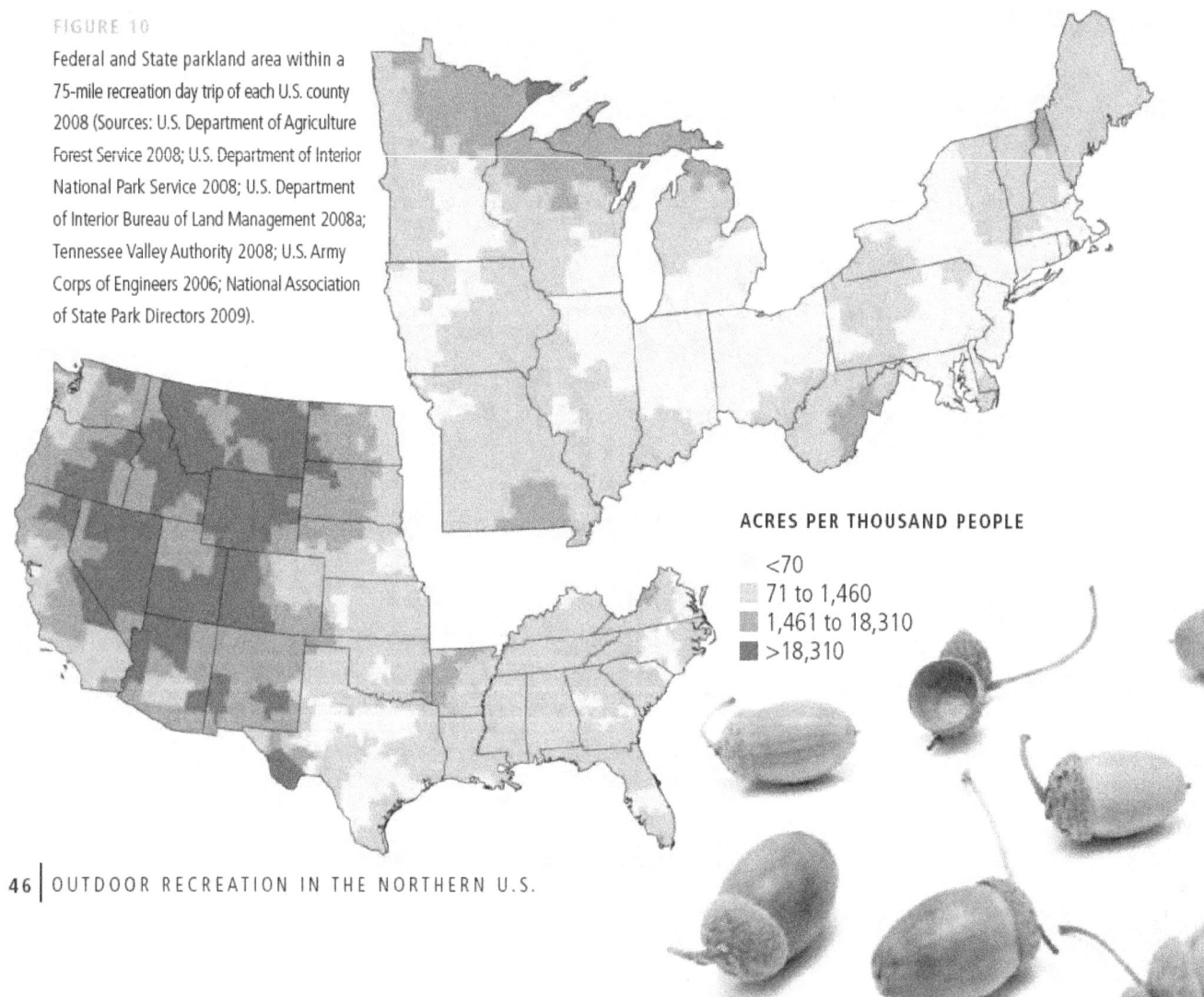

ACRES PER THOUSAND PEOPLE

<70
71 to 1,460
1,461 to 18,310
>18,310

in southern Missouri, eastern West Virginia, and northern New Hampshire. Cook County in the Boundary Waters of Minnesota, is the only Northern county in the most abundant category of more than 18,310 acres per 1,000 people.

Non-Federal forests—Residents of the drier counties of western Texas and some parts of Nevada and California lack non-Federal forest land within a 75-mile recreation day trip zone (Fig. 11). Although all northern counties have access to non-Federal forest within the zone, the most abundant non-Federal forests are in northern Minnesota, Wisconsin, Michigan, and much of Maine. In addition to having large forest acreage, these areas are sparsely populated, which means that they have the most non-Federal forest acres per person. With the exception of Missouri, most of the midwestern area is in the category of less than 1,330 acres per 1,000 people. Not surprisingly, the northeastern urban corridor is also in the least abundant category.

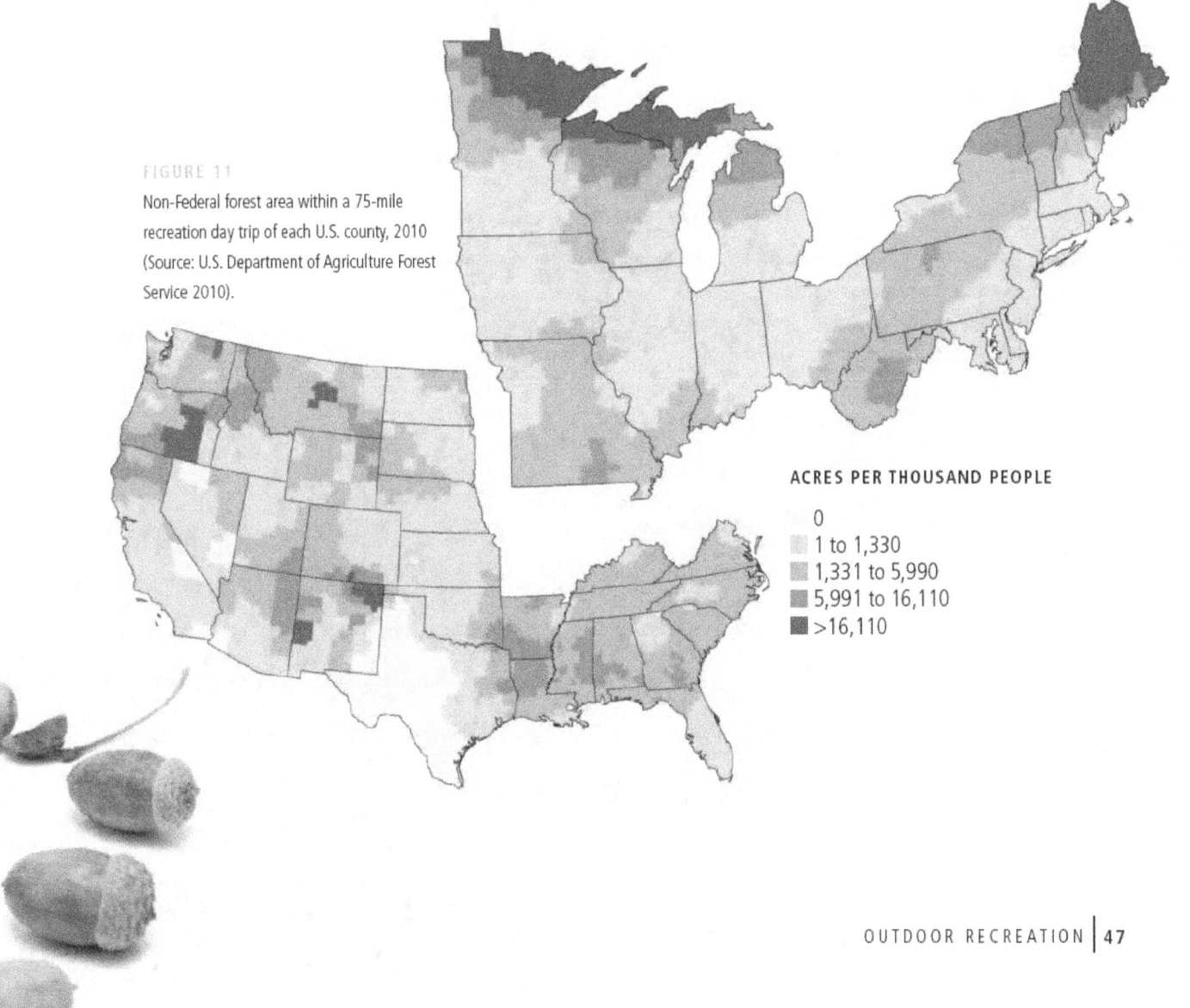

FIGURE 11

Non-Federal forest area within a 75-mile recreation day trip of each U.S. county, 2010 (Source: U.S. Department of Agriculture Forest Service 2010).

ACRES PER THOUSAND PEOPLE

0
1 to 1,330
1,331 to 5,990
5,991 to 16,110
>16,110

Water—As with public land area, all counties have access to some water area when the 75-mile zone for each county is considered (Fig. 12). Water as defined here is all water area with the exception of open ocean. For the North, greater water area per capita is in the same Great Lakes region of Minnesota, Wisconsin, and Michigan that is abundant in Federal and State parkland and non-Federal forests. The counties of eastern Maine are also among the Nation's most abundant in water acres per capita. Among the least abundant are the Kansas City and St. Louis metropolitan areas, a large portion of central and western central Iowa, and a large band of counties stretching from eastern Illinois all the way to the New York metropolitan area.

FORECASTS OF FUTURE AVAILABILITY

Federal and State parkland—Federal and State parkland area is expected to be constant or almost constant through time. Nearly 30 percent of the total U.S. land and water area is in Federal or State management, which is slightly more than 2 acres per person (Table 23). Because of population growth, per capita Federal and State park acreage is predicted to decrease to 1.4 acres per person (or about 68 percent of the 2008 amount) by 2060.

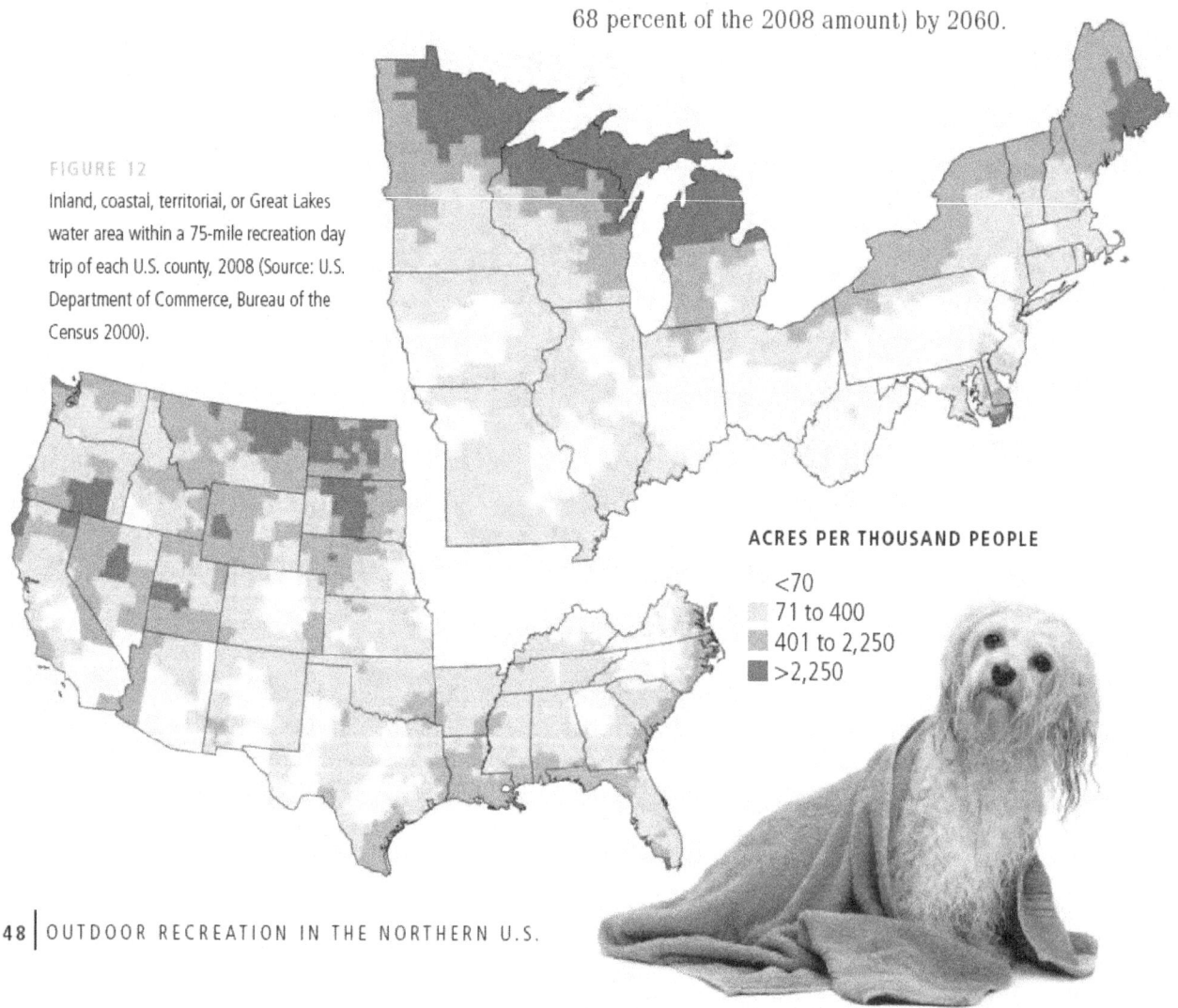

FIGURE 12

Inland, coastal, territorial, or Great Lakes water area within a 75-mile recreation day trip of each U.S. county, 2008 (Source: U.S. Department of Commerce, Bureau of the Census 2000).

ACRES PER THOUSAND PEOPLE

<70
71 to 400
401 to 2,250
>2,250

Table 23—Projected change in total acres and per capita acres of federal and State parkland with percent of total surface area 2008, projected per capita acres 2060, and percent of 2008 acres projected for 2060, by region (not including AK or HI) (Sources: U.S. Department of Agriculture Forest Service 2008, 2009b; U.S. Department of the Interior National Park Service 2008; U.S. Department of the Interior Fish and Wildlife Service 2008; U.S. Department of the Interior Bureau of Land Management 2008; Tennessee Valley Authority 2008; U.S. Army Corps of Engineers 2006.).

| Region | Federal and state park land[a] | | | | |
| | 2008 | | | 2060 | |
	Acres (thousands)	Percent of total area	Per capita acres	Projected per capita acres	Percent of 2008 acres projected for 2060
North	19,915	4.2	0.16	0.13	79
South	28,274	5.0	0.28	0.17	63
Rocky Mountains	259,643	34.6	9.35	5.22	56
Pacific Coast	319,487	49.5	6.51	4.19	64
U.S. total	627,319	25.8	2.06	1.40	68

[a]*Federal and State parkland is the sum of federal land-managing agency area and state park system areas. Federal agencies include NPS, USFS, USFWS, BLM, TVA, and USACE. USDI Bureau of Reclamation not included because most of its areas are managed by other agencies.*

In the North, the Federal or State parkland area per person is projected to decrease to 0.13 acres, about 79 percent of the 2008 level. Compared to their western counterparts, the Eastern States currently have relatively little Federal or State parkland; for example, the North region has only 4.2 percent of national total, which is less than 0.2 acres per person. The percentage of total area that is Federal or State parkland is slightly higher and the population is lower in the north central area than in the northeastern area, but both areas are projected to have the same rate of population growth through 2060 as the North region overall.

Non-Federal forests—Non-Federal forest land area is expected to continue to be converted to developed uses. Excluding Alaska and Hawaii, about 19 percent of total U.S. surface area is non-Federal forest (Table 24), which is about 1.27 acres per person. By 2060, per capita non-Federal forest area is predicted to decrease to 0.8 acres per person, about 63 percent of the current level. In the North, more than 31 percent of total land area is non-Federal forest, which is the highest percent of any region (just slightly ahead of the South). Given the current North population, this represents about 1.19 acres per person. By 2060, per capita non-Federal forest is predicted to decrease to 0.88 acres per person, or 74 percent of the current level.

The percentage of total area that is non-Federal forest is much higher for the northeastern area (53 percent) than for the north central area (22 percent). However, given differences in population growth, projected per capita acreages in each area will be nearly the same by 2060, with both at 0.88 acres per person.

Table 24—Projected change in total and per capita acres of non-Federal forest land by region for the contiguous United States from 2010 to 2060 (not including AK and HI) (Source: U.S. Department of Agriculture, Forest Service 2010).

Region	Non-Federal forest land				
	2010			2060	
	Total acres (thousands)	Percent of total area	Per capita acres	Projected per capita acres	Percent of 2010 acres projected for 2060
North	147,762	31.4	1.19	0.88	74
South	171,810	30.5	1.66	0.95	57
Rocky Mountains	28,486	3.8	1.02	0.55	54
Pacific Coast	37,736	17.1	0.79	0.47	59
U.S. total	385,793	19.3	1.27	0.80	63

Water—Like Federal and State parkland, total water area is expected to be constant or almost constant through time. About 7 percent of total U.S. surface area is water, which roughly equates to a half acre per person (Table 25).

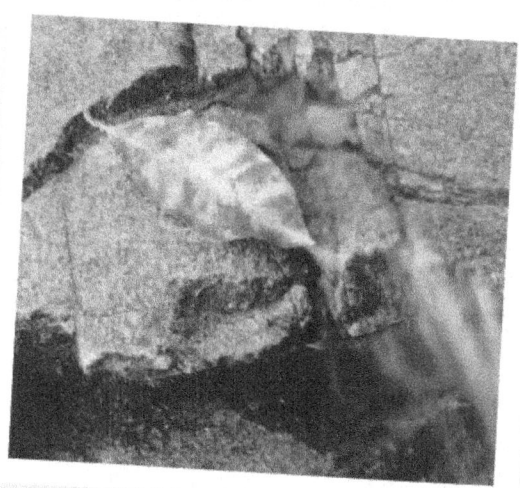

For the North, which is heavily influenced by the Great Lakes, water area is 0.46 acres per person, or more than 12 percent of the total surface area (slightly more than the Pacific Coast and a lot more than the other two regions). By 2060, per capita water is predicted to decrease to 0.36 acres, 79 percent of the 2008 level. Water as a percent of total surface area is slightly higher in the north central (12.9 percent) than in the northeastern area (10.2 percent). Per capita water acreages for the north central area (0.55 acres per capita) are projected to remain much larger than in the northeastern area (0.18 acres per capita), although both areas expect population to grow at the same rate.

Table 25—Projected change in inland, coastal, territorial, and Great Lakes water area from 2008 to 2060, by region (not including AK or HI) (Source: U.S. Department of Commerce, Bureau of the Census 2000).

| Region | Water area | | | | |
| | 2008 | | | 2060 | |
	Acres (thousands)	Percent of total area	Per capita acres	Projected per capita acres	Percent of 2008 acres projected for 2060
North	56,834	12.1	0.46	0.36	79
South	29,282	5.2	0.28	0.18	63
Rocky Mountains	7,289	1.0	0.26	0.15	56
Pacific Coast	70,848	11.0	1.44	0.93	64
U.S. total	164,253	6.8	0.54	0.37	68

Summary of Key Findings
POPULATION

- From 1990 to 2009, total population in the North grew at a rate (11 percent) that was less than half the national rate (23 percent). The region has just under 40 percent (14.9 million) of the country's African American population and ranks second to the Pacific Coast in Asian/Pacific Islander population, which had more than doubled (123 percent) in the North. The Hispanic population almost exactly doubled to about 11.1 million.

- The South and the Rocky Mountains were the only regions to outpace the national growth rate for every single age group. In the North, the Baby Boomer age groups ranging from 45 to 64 have dominated all others in percentage growth from 1990 to 2009, but the rate of growth for this group lagged behind the rest of the Nation. Modest decreases occurred in the North for the younger than 6 age group and held constant for 6- to-10-year-olds. Interestingly, the 25- to 34-age group decreased by nearly 17 percent, which far exceeded decreases in other regions and for the Nation as a whole. This phenomenon was likely a function, in part, of early-career individuals seeking employment opportunities elsewhere. The rate of growth of people age 65 and older in the North (14 percent) was less than half that of the other regions and the Nation, where the growth was 27 percent.

- The North is known for its cluster of high-density metropolitan counties that stretch from greater Washington and Baltimore to southern Maine. Major cities include Philadelphia, New York, and Boston. Other high-density areas include many of the rust belt cities of Pennsylvania and Ohio; most of southern Michigan; the large urban corridor stretching from Gary, IN, through metropolitan Chicago and north to Milwaukee; the Minnesota Twin Cities of Minneapolis and St. Paul; greater Indianapolis; and the two urban regions of Missouri, St. Louis, and Kansas City. The highest growth in population density (persons per square mile) from 1990 to 2009 occurred in the Washington-to-Boston urban corridor and in the Greater Chicago and Twin Cities areas. Although counties located in suburban areas of the largest cities grew, the urban cores of metropolitan Detroit, Cleveland, Cincinnati, St. Louis, and Buffalo, NY, all lost population. Losses also occurred in much of Pennsylvania, West Virginia, New York, Iowa, and northern Missouri.

- With moderate growth, the total population of the United States is projected to exceed 447 million by 2060, an increase of almost 46 percent. Projected growth for the North is expected to be 26 percent, much less than the other three regions. The 12 States and the District of Columbia in the northeastern area and the eight States in the north central area are all expected to grow at virtually the same rate. New Hampshire, Maryland, and Vermont have the largest projected growth, and the smallest growth rate is expected for New York, West Virginia, and Ohio. Washington, D.C.'s population is projected to decrease almost 17 percent.

RECREATION DEMAND

- One overriding recreation trend is that the relative popularity of outdoor activities is shifting over time. For example, the number of people participating in wildlife or birdwatching and photography is growing while numbers participating in some other activities are not.

- For the North, rate of growth of total outdoor recreation participants and total activity days was lower than the national rate. For those age 16 and older, participation increased about 4 percent, from about 90 to 94 million, and participation days increased by 24 percent in the last decade. Average participation days per person across the full list of 60 activities rose from about 300 per year to 359, a 20 percent increase. Some of the slower gains can be attributed to the North's lower population growth rate compared to the Nation as a whole.

- Of the most popular activities in the North (those having over 30 million participants), the top six slots were occupied by walking for pleasure, attending family gatherings outdoors, gardening or landscaping, viewing/photographing natural scenery, visiting outdoor nature centers, and picnicking.

Other popular growth activities included viewing/photographing flowers and trees, viewing/photographing wildlife (besides birds and fish), visiting a beach, and viewing/photographing birds. Activities oriented toward viewing and photographing nature (scenery, flowers/trees/other plants, birds, and wildlife) have been among the fastest growing in popularity.

- Among moderately popular activities (10 to 30 million participants), the most popular were viewing or photographing fish, warm water fishing, motor boating, and visiting a waterside (besides a beach). Growth has been especially strong for off-highway-vehicle driving, warm water fishing, and viewing or photographing fish.

- In the 3 to 10 million participant category, backpacking and ice skating have both been declining over the past 10 years, indicating continuing shifts in activity popularity. Kayaking was the fastest growing of these activities by a wide margin, followed by snowboarding, caving, and water skiing. Several activities posted decreases during this decade.

- Only six activities attracted fewer than 3 million participants, led by orienteering (which grew by over 90 percent in the last decade), snowshoeing, and migratory bird hunting. These are primarily niche activities that appeal to specialized segments of recreation participants.

- Just under three-fourths of northern 6-to-19-year-olds spent 2 or more hours outdoors on a typical weekend day (58 percent on a weekday). Forty-three percent spent 4 or more hours outdoors on weekend days (26 percent on weekdays).

- Among young people 6 to 19 years old, unstructured free play or "hanging out" and biking/jogging/walking/skateboarding were the leading outdoor activities, each with more than 78 percent participation. Slightly more than half of respondents used electronic devices while they were outdoors, presumably much of it during unstructured time.

- Among 6- to 19-year-olds, structured nature-based activities, such as attending outdoor camps, classes, and field trips, attracted about 36 percent. Approximately 30 percent also participated in a variety of nature-based recreation activities, such as swimming, diving, snorkeling, birdwatching, wildlife viewing, hiking, camping, and fishing.

PUBLIC RECREATION RESOURCES

- Compared to the more than 92 percent of Federal land that is located in the West, less than 3 percent, about 17.9 million acres, is in the North and about 69 percent of that is managed by the Forest Service.

- Although Federal acreage changes very little over time, population changes a great deal. In the North, which had an 8 percent decrease, Federal acres per 1,000 persons decreased more slowly than the national rate of decrease (-14 percent since 1995).

- The North accounts for just 1.5 percent of the land area in the National Wilderness Preservation System, about 1.7 million of the over 109 million acres nationally. Modest additions to the system in the North since 1995 resulted in a 1.5 percent increase in wilderness acres per capita.

- Nearly 2,200 miles of National Wild and Scenic River miles are in the North (about 17 percent of all designated river miles), representing a 6.0 percent increase in protected river miles since 2000 (less than the national growth rate of 11 percent).

- The North has more than 7,300 National Recreation Trail System miles, more than any other region and about 36 percent of the system nationally. The addition of 3,200 miles (78 percent) since 2004 was higher than any other region except the South. The region has fewer than 10 Federal recreation facilities per million people, or about 1 per 105,000 people. After camping, boating is the most common Federal recreation facility.

- State park system areas total nearly 5.2 million acres in the North. Throughout the region, especially New England and the rest of the Northeastern States, State park resources are situated within an hour's drive of home for most people.

- Nationwide, more than 8,800 local governments provide recreation and park services. Nearly half (48.3 percent) of these local units were in the North, where the number of local parks and recreation departments per million people was up almost 14 percent since 1997—very close to the national growth rate of 13 percent. Some local government agencies have specific mandates to manage for conservation and compatible nature-based recreation.
- On average, residents of the North have access to fewer than 1,460 acres of public land per 1,000 people (or 1.5 acres per person) within 75 miles of their homes.
- Within a 75-mile recreation day trip zone, the greatest water (non-ocean) area per capita is in counties located near the Great Lakes.
- The North has relatively more non-Federal forest land along the Appalachian Mountains, in southern Illinois, much of Missouri, and similar to water, is most abundant in Maine and northern Minnesota, Wisconsin, and Michigan. On a per capita basis, most of the metropolitan areas have relatively little forest land close by.

- In the North, the Federal and State parkland area per person is projected to decrease to 0.13 acres, about 79 percent of the 2008 level, by 2060. Because the northern population is not projected to grow as fast as the Nation or any other region, the projected decrease per capita is lower.
- Currently, more than 31 percent of total land area in the North is non-Federal forest, or 1.19 acres per person. By 2060, per capita non-Federal forest is predicted to decrease to 0.88 acres per person, or 74 percent of the 2010 level, lower than all other regions and the Nation as a whole.
- Total water area, like Federal and State parkland, is expected to stay mostly constant over the next several decades. Currently, water area in the North is slightly more than 12 percent of the region's total surface area, or 0.46 acres per person. By 2060, per capita water is predicted to decrease to 0.36 acres per person, or 79 percent of the 2008 level. Similar to the other resources, the projected reduction in water resources per capita is less for the North than for the Nation and all other regions.

Discussion of Findings

The North has been and continues to be a socially dynamic region of the country. It is a region characterized by large metropolitan areas, population diversity, steady projected population growth, and a mixture of public and private land and water resources. In the last two decades, the North's population grew at a considerably slower rate than the Nation as a whole. Growth has been moderated by many of the region's older people having moved to warmer climates and many of its younger people having moved in search of better employment opportunities.

Even though growth is slower than in other regions, the large population of the North means numerous densely populated communities, large commercial areas, and a wide array of industrial complexes. Many areas have changed radically to accommodate communities and their infrastructure, leaving only a fraction of the natural lands that once dominated the landscape.

At the same time, more individuals, families, and other households translate into greater demand for venues for outdoor recreation. This rising demand presents a dilemma for the North's shrinking supply of undeveloped lands. Will these lands and the developed parks of the future North be sufficient to meet public expectations?

Not only is recreation demand growing, but also what people now choose as outdoor activities is shifting from what they were in past decades and generations. Similar to some of the relatively new activities like orienteering, snowboarding, and mountain biking, which were largely unknown to past generations, new outdoor activities will undoubtedly emerge as the 21st century continues to unfold. One very prominent factor driving this emergence is the changed and ever changing relationship between young people and the outdoors. Contrary to the widely held notion that children in today's United States are not spending time outdoors, the National Kids Survey results suggest that they may actually spend quite a bit of time outdoors, even though significant numbers are using electronic devices when doing so.

Today's youth are tomorrow's adults. How they spend their time now will carry over to affect their future adult lifestyles. Certainly, they have different interests than their parents' generation. The experiences and opportunities of today's young people are different. Likewise, the next generation will be different than the youth of today. If history is a predictor of the future, generational differences will continue to be major drivers of change. This will very likely influence the way people think about and use the outdoors. Undoubtedly, this future use will involve electronic devices, and who can know what these may be in 20 years.

Concurrent with population growth and shifting recreation demands is a very strong likelihood of increasing pressure on forest and other undeveloped lands. Especially in the North, this poses a challenge. Because of high population densities, the average resident of most northern counties has access to fewer than 1.5 acres of Federal or State land within 75 miles of his or her residence. As well, many of the major metropolitan areas have relatively little access to nearby non-Federal forest land, and recreationally accessible water is becoming increasingly scarce throughout much of the region. Like public lands, total water area is fairly static over time; with increasing population, this translates into decreasing per capita acreage in future years.

Population, recreation, and resource trends are all headed in directions that leave one wondering. Who will be the future recreation participants from among the North's growing and changing population? Will participants of the future be representative of the growing diversity of this region's population? Or, could there be a narrowing of participants' demographics as a result of increasing per capita scarcity of places and resources for outdoor recreation?

Where will outdoor recreation occur in the future? As land and water resources in rural areas are increasingly pressured by expanding urban and other development uses, private land and water are likely to become less available for outdoor recreation for some segments of the population. This raises the question of how future residents of the North may gain access to outdoor recreation areas. If the importance of easily accessible, nearby public or private outdoor resources increases in the future, recreation and other nontangible benefits could become important factors in land-value calculations, especially in areas close to population centers. Without inclusion of the value of recreation and other ecosystem services in land value calculations, development value will almost always outweigh other considerations. Including recreation and other ecosystem service values perhaps would open an opportunity for local citizenry and public service organizations to offer incentives that would encourage private owners to keep more land in forest and make it more accessible.

*Autumn colors
in the forest*

Acknowledgments

Thank you to our reviewers John Daigle, Associate Professor of Forest Recreation Management at The University of Maine, Orono, ME; and Rob Porter, Professor in Recreation, Park, and Tourism Administration at Western Illinois University, Macomb, IL. We also thank Susan Wright, Carol Whitlock, and Rhonda Cobourn, who provided editorial guidance and support.

We thank them all

Literature Cited

American Trails. 2010. National recreation trails database. Redding, CA: American Trails. http://www.americantrails.org/NRTDatabase/index.php or http://tutsan.forest.net/trails/. (22 February 2010).

Clawson, M.; Knetsch, J.L. 1966. Economics of outdoor recreation. Baltimore, MD: Resources for the Future. 328 p.

Cordell, H.K. 2008. The latest on trends in nature-based outdoor recreation. Forest History Today. Spring: 4-10.

Cordell, H.K.; Betz, C.J.; Green, G.T. 2008. Nature-based outdoor recreation trends and wilderness. International Journal of Wilderness. 14(2): 7-13.

Cordell, H.K.; Betz, C.J.; Green, G.T.; Mou, S.; Leeworthy, V.R.; Wiley, P.C.; Barry, J.J.; Hellerstein, D. 2004. Outdoor recreation for 21st century America. State College, PA: Venture Publishing, Inc. 293 p.

Cordell, H.K. 2012. Outdoor recreation trends and futures: a technical document supporting the Forest Service 2010 RPA Assessment. Gen. Tech. Rep. SRS-150. Asheville, NC: U.S. Department of Agriculture Forest Service, Southern Research Station. 167 p.

Daigle, J.J.; Utley, L.; Chase, L.C.; Kuentzel, W.F.; Brown, T.L. 2012. Does new large private landownership and their management priorities influence public access in the northern forest? Journal of Forestry. 110(2): 89-96.

Franklin, R.S. 2003. Domestic migration across regions, divisions, and states: 1995 to 2000. Washington, DC: U.S. Department of Commerce, Economics and Statistics Administration, Census Bureau. http://www.census.gov/prod/2003pubs/censr-7.pdf. (17 October 2011).

Interagency Wild and Scenic Rivers Council. 2009. River mileage classifications for components of the national wild and scenic rivers system. Washington, DC: Interagency Wild and Scenic Rivers Coordinating Council. http://www.rivers.gov/publications/rivers-table.pdf. (23 February 2010).

Larson, L.R.; Green, G.T.; Cordell, H.K. 2011. Children's time outdoors: results and implications of the national kids survey. Journal of Park and Recreation Administration. 29(2): 1-20.

National Association of State Park Directors. 1996. Annual information exchange for the period July 1, 1994 through June 30, 1995. On file with: North Carolina State University, Department of Parks, Recreation and Tourism Management, Jordan Hall 5107, Box 7106, Raleigh, NC 27697-7106. (Yu-Fai Leung, principal investigator).

National Association of State Park Directors. 2009. Annual information exchange for the period July 1, 2007 through June 30, 2008. On file with: North Carolina State University, Department of Parks, Recreation and Tourism Management, Jordan Hall 5107, Box 7106, Raleigh, NC 27697-7106. (Yu-Fai Leung, principal investigator).

Outdoor Recreation Resources Review Commission. 1962. National recreation survey. ORRRC Study Report 19. Washington, DC: Outdoor Recreation Resources Review Commission. http://www.srs.fs.usda.gov/trends/Nsre/orrrc.html. (30 June 2011).

Shifley, S.R.; Aguilar, F.X.; Song, N.; Stewart, S.I.; Nowak, D.J.; Gormanson, D.D.; Moser, W.K.; Wormstead, S.; Greenfield, E.J. 2012. Forests of the Northern United States. Gen. Tech. Rep. NRS-90. Newtown Square, PA: U.S. Department of Agriculture, Forest Service, Northern Research Station. 202 p.

Tennessee Valley Authority. 2008. Recreation resources inventory database. On file with: Tennessee Valley Authority, 400 West Summit Hill Drive, Knoxville, TN 37902.

U.S. Army Corps of Engineers. 2006. Value to the nation: recreation fast facts. http://www.corpsresults.us/recreation/recfastfacts.asp. (1 April 2009).

U.S. Department of Agriculture Forest Service. 1995. Land areas report as of September 30, 1995. On file with: U.S. Department of Agriculture Forest Service, Lands and Realty Management Office, 1400 Independence Ave., SW, Mailstop 1124, Washington, DC 20250-1124.

U.S. Department of Agriculture Forest Service. 2008. Land areas report as of September 30, 2008. Washington, DC: U.S. Department of Agriculture, Forest Service. http://www.fs.fed.us/land/staff/lar/. (9 February 2009).

U.S. Department of Agriculture Forest Service. 2009a. National survey on recreation and the environment [NSRE Dataset]. On file with: U.S. Department of Agriculture Forest Service, Southern Research Station, Recreation, Wilderness, Urban Forest, and Demographic Trends Research Group, 320 Green St., Athens, GA 30602-2044.

U.S. Department of Agriculture Forest Service. 2009b. State park systems database compiled from published state literature and state park Web sites. On file with: U.S. Department of Agriculture Forest Service, Southern Research Station, Recreation, Wilderness, Urban Forest, and Demographic Trends Research Group, 320 Green St., Athens, GA 30602-2044.

U.S. Department of Agriculture Forest Service. 2010. RPA Assessment land use projections. On file with: U.S. Department of Agriculture Forest Service, Southern Research Station, Forest Economics and Policy, P.O. Box 12254, Research Triangle Park, NC 27709.

U.S. Department of Commerce, Bureau of the Census. 1990. Census of population and housing. 1990. Summary tape file 1. http://www2.census.gov/census_1990/1990STF1.html#1A. Washington, DC: U.S. Department of Commerce, Bureau of the Census. (23 September 2009).

U.S. Department of Commerce, Census Bureau. 2000. Census 2000 U.S. gazetteer files, water area (square miles). Washington, DC: U.S. Department of Commerce, Bureau of Census. http://www.census.gov/geo/www/gazetteer/places2k.html. (20 June 2005).

U.S. Department of Commerce, Census Bureau. 2007a. Census of governments, government employment and payroll, local government, 1997 and 2007. Washington, DC: U.S. Department of Commerce, Census Bureau. http://www.census.gov/govs/apes/. (31 March 2009).

U.S. Department of Commerce, Census Bureau. 2007b. Economic census, county business patterns, 1998 and 2007. Washington, DC: U.S. Department of Commerce, Bureau of Census. http://www.census.gov/econ/cbp/index.html. (24 August 2009).

U.S. Department of Commerce, Census Bureau. 2009a. SC-EST2009-alldata6: annual state resident population estimates for 6 race groups (5 race alone groups and one group with two or more race groups) by age, sex, and Hispanic origin: April 1, 2000 to July 1, 2009. Washington, DC: U.S. Department of Commerce, Bureau of Census. http://www.census.gov/compendia/statab/2011/tables/11s0019.xls . (9 January 2012).

U.S. Department of Commerce, Census Bureau. 2009b. CC-EST2009-ALLDATA-[ST-FIPS]: annual county resident population estimates by age, sex, race, and Hispanic origin: April 1, 2000 to July 1, 2009. Washington, DC: U.S. Department of Commerce, Bureau of Census. http://www.census.gov/popest/data/counties/asrh/2009/CC-EST2009-alldata.html . (9 January 2012).

U.S. Department of the Interior. 2009. Recreation one-stop initiative: recreation information data base. Washington, DC: U.S. Department of Interior. https://www.recdata.gov/RIDBWeb/ Controller.jpf. (3 April).

U.S. Department of the Interior, Bureau of Land Management. 1994. Public land statistics 1993. Vol. 178. Washington, DC: U.S. Department of Interior.

U.S. Department of the Interior, Bureau of Land Management. 2008. Public land statistics 2008. Washington, DC: U.S. Department of Interior, Bureau of Land Management. http://www.blm.gov/public_land_statistics/pls08/index.htm. (23 June 2009).

U.S. Department of the Interior, Bureau of Reclamation. 1993. Recreation fast facts. On file with: U.S. Department of the Interior, Bureau of Reclamation, Land & Mineral Records System, 1849 C St., NW, Rm. 5625, Washington, DC 20240.

U.S. Department of the Interior, Bureau of Reclamation. 2008. Recreation fast facts. Washington, DC: U.S. Department of Interior, Bureau of Reclamation. http://www.usbr.gov/recreation. (19 February 2009).

U.S. Department of the Interior, Fish and Wildlife Service. 1995. Annual report of lands as of September 30, 1995. On file with: U.S. Department of the Interior, Fish and Wildlife Service, 4401 N. Fairfax Dr., Arlington, VA 22203.

U.S. Department of the Interior, Fish and Wildlife Service. 2008. Annual report of lands as of September 30, 2008. Washington, DC: U.S. Department of Interior, Fish and Wildlife Service. http://www.fws.gov/refuges/land/LandReport.html. (18 June 2009).

U.S. Department of the Interior, National Park Service. 1995. Listing of acreage by state and county as of 10/31/95. On file with: U.S. Department of the Interior, National Park Service, Land Resources Division, 1849 C St., NW, Washington, DC 20240.

U.S. Department of the Interior, National Park Service. 2008. Listing of acreage by state and county as of 12/31/2008. http://www.nature.nps.gov/stats/acreagemenu.cfm. (26 February 2009).

Wilderness.net. 2009. Wilderness data search. Missoula, MT: Wilderness Institute. http://www.wilderness.net/index.cfm?fuse=NWPS&sec=advSearch. (6 July).

Woods & Poole Economics, Inc. 2009. 2010 complete economic and demographic data source (CEDDS). Washington, DC: Woods & Poole. [CD-ROM].

Yang, T.; Snyder, A.R. 2007. Population change in the Northeast, 2000-2005. State College, PA: University of Pennsylvania. http://nercrd.psu.edu/Publications/rdppapers/rdp39.pdf. (17 October 2011).

Zarnoch, S.J.; Cordell, H.K.; Betz, C.J.; Bergstrom, J.C. 2010. Multiple imputation: an application to income nonresponse in the national survey on recreation and the environment. Res. Pap. SRS–49. Asheville, NC: U.S. Department of Agriculture Forest Service, Southern Research Station. 15 p.

Seedling growth
on forest floor

66

Appendix

Methods and Data Sources
POPULATION AND DEMOGRAPHIC TRENDS AND PROJECTED FUTURES

Historical data from the 1990 U.S. Census of Population and Housing through the 2009 census population estimates were analyzed to examine recent trends in population, population distribution, and demographic composition. National and regional population totals and percents are presented in tables, along with maps showing the distribution of the population among northern counties. All maps show four shading levels that correspond to the following percentage distributions of the data depicted in each map: 0 to 35, 36 to 70, 71 to 90, and 91 to 100. The two highest percentage ranges (shown by the darkest shades) are purposely more restricted to emphasize counties having the largest counts of population or more significant data values.

Included in this report are data on population by race/ethnicity, population by age groups, current population density (persons per square mile), change in population density since 1990, percentage change in Hispanic population, percentage change in non-Hispanic White population, and projected changes in population density from 2008 to 2060. For comparison with the North, the same statistics are also shown for all counties of the rest of the country, except for Hawaii and Alaska. The northern region consists of Connecticut, Delaware, District of Columbia, Illinois, Indiana, Iowa, Maine, Maryland, Massachusetts, Michigan, Minnesota, Missouri, New Hampshire, New Jersey, New York, Ohio, Pennsylvania, Rhode Island, Vermont, West Virginia and Wisconsin.

The U.S. Department of Commerce, Bureau of the Census provides updated annual population estimates for the Nation, States, and counties each year. Based on these updates, county-scale maps were produced for this report showing change in Hispanic and other segments of the North's population. (The census released preliminary 2010 estimates of total population by county in March 2011, but had not released population estimates by demographic categories at the time of writing.) Data consulted included:

U.S. Department of Commerce, Bureau of the Census (2009a), SC-EST2009-alldata6: Annual State Resident Population Estimates for 6 Race Groups (5 Race Alone Groups and One Group with Two or more Race Groups) by Age, Sex, and Hispanic Origin: April 1, 2000 to July 1, 2009 (http://www.census.gov/compendia/statab/2011/tables/11s0019.xls)

U.S. Department of Commerce, Bureau of the Census (2009b), CC-EST2009-ALLDATA-[ST-FIPS]: Annual County Resident Population Estimates by Age, Sex, Race, and Hispanic Origin: April 1, 2000 to July 1, 2009 (http://www.census.gov/popest/data/counties/asrh/2009/CC-EST2009-alldata.html)

State and county population from the 1990 census were derived from Woods & Poole Economics, Inc. (2009).

Working from Census Bureau estimates, the U.S. Department of Agriculture-Forest Service Southern Research Station developed county-scale forecasts of population change for three of the future scenarios defined by the International Panel on Climate Change in its Fourth Assessment Report (Zarnoch et al. 2010). The scenarios—labeled A1B, A2, and B2—were adapted for use in both the national 2010 Renewable Resources Planning Act (RPA) Assessment (Cordell 2012) and for the Northern Forest Futures Project, currently underway at the Forest Service (Northern Research Station, Eastern Region, Forest Products Laboratory, and Northeastern Area State and Private Forestry) in partnership with the Northeastern Area Association of State Foresters and the University of Missouri. The overall purpose for examining population change in the context of these scenarios is to evaluate the sensitivity of forest and other resource trends to a range of feasible futures. In this report, percentage change over the 50-year assessment period (2010 to 2060) is shown only for the A1B moderate population growth scenario. Under this scenario, total population in the United States is projected to exceed 447 million people by 2060, a growth of almost 46 percent.

RECREATION ACTIVITY TREND DATA

The source of data on recreation activity trends for adults is the National Survey on Recreation and the Environment (NSRE). Sponsored by the Southern Research Station, the University of Georgia and the University of Tennessee, it is a general population random-digit-dialed telephone survey that asks Americans age 16 and older about their participation in outdoor recreation activities (U.S. Department of Agriculture Forest Service 2009a). The NSRE data presented here are from surveys conducted continuously from 1999 to 2009, with a brief interruption during 2004.

Earlier estimates of trends in outdoor recreation in general and in nature-based outdoor recreation in particular (Cordell 2008) were conducted for the RPA Assessment. This report updates those findings. NSRE data were pooled to define two trend periods: 1999 to 2001 and 2005 to 2009. (The volume of NSRE surveying decreased in the latter years which resulted in smaller yearly sample sizes and thus the combining of more years in the later period.) An overview of Americans' participation in outdoor recreation in general was constructed by defining a "participant" as any person who engaged in at least one of 60 outdoor recreation activities one or more times during the 12 months prior to the date they were interviewed. A "yes" value was assigned to respondents if they reported participation in any of the 60 activities, with "no" indicating

that the individual did not participate in any activity during the past year. A similar indicator was used to determine nature-based activity participation using a shorter list of 50 activities that typically occur in natural settings. Previous estimates from the 1994-to-1995 period are included to indicate overall trends across two decades.

The source of data for youth time in the outdoors is the National Kids Survey (Cordell 2012), a household telephone survey that was conducted by the Southern Research Station in cooperation with the University of Tennessee and the University of Georgia from 2007 to 2011. Households with a 6- to 19-year-old qualified to participate. If a household had more than one qualifying household member, the survey questions were directed to the individual with the most recent birthday. Teenagers 16 to 19 responded for themselves; an adult proxy, usually a parent, answered for children age 6 to 15. The survey data were post-weighted to approximate census population percents by gender and by eight age strata. Questions asked included the amount of time spent outdoors regardless of activity, as well as the types of activities engaged in. A total of 1,945 respondents or their proxies participated, 763 from Northern States.

RECREATION RESOURCE DATA

Federal resources—The Federal land managing agencies are the sources for Federal outdoor recreation resources data. The four largest Federal land-managing agencies—Forest Service and the U.S. Department of the Interior Bureau of Land Management, Fish and Wildlife Service, and National Park Service—have real estate offices that maintain records on the size, location, and boundaries of their holdings. The three Federal water resources management agencies—U.S. Army Corps of Engineers, U.S. Department of the Interior Bureau of Reclamation, and Tennessee Valley Authority—have much smaller land holdings.

Resources protected by inclusion in the National Wilderness Preservation System, the National Wild and Scenic River System, and the National Trails System are also described in this paper in the section titled specially designated Federal land systems. Current and past data from each of these systems was examined for trends in per capita availability.

Federal recreation sites and facilities are cataloged in an online database called the Recreation Information Database, better known through its portal as www.recreation.gov [Date accessed: December 15, 2011] or simply rec. gov. The Department of the Interior coordinates an interagency coalition that gathers recreation site and facilities information across all Federal agencies. The rec.gov Web site includes a standardized list of 22 separate recreation activities, facilities, or attractions with binary (yes/no) availability. Trend data are not available for this database because it is fairly new, originating around 2002. Both a limitation and a strength of the Recreation Information Database is that it is an evolving source of information, which is expanding and growing, but not yet complete across Federal recreation facilities.

State resources—Two sources of State park system data were used in this report. First is the National Association of State Park Directors Annual Information Exchange survey, which collects data from all 50 State park systems. This report uses survey data to assess the status of each State park system's resources, operations, and visits. Included in coverage are State parks, recreation areas, natural areas, historical areas, environmental education areas, scientific areas, forests, wildlife and fish areas, and other miscellaneous areas. The exchange summarizes all information by State; it does not have individual State park unit information, such as size, location, and site attributes. The most consistent data over the history of the exchange have been about the State park and State recreation area classifications.

The second source is a State park database of individual park system units developed from printed and online sources[1], and includes acreage data and location (latitude/longitude coordinates). The database focuses on the three most common types of State park system units: parks, recreation areas, and historic sites.

Local government resources—The data source for local government outdoor recreation resources is the Census Bureau Census of Governments, which is conducted every 5 years. The classifications for this census are type of governmental unit and services provided. A difficulty in assessing local government recreation resources is the sheer number and variety of local jurisdictions that provide park and recreation services. Further, many local agencies place as much (and sometimes more) emphasis on indoor leisure programs and services as on outdoor resources. The Census of Governments does not provide details on land holdings or other resources; rather it collects administrative, financial, and employment data. This report assumes that all local government agencies listed as providing recreation and park services also include management of some outdoor recreation resources, although the amount provided is not known.

---

[1] Cordell, H. Ken. 2011. [Untitled]. Unpublished database. On file with: Pioneering Research Project, Southern Research Station, U.S. Department of Agriculture Forest Service, 320 Green Street, Athens, GA 30602-2044.

Private Recreation Businesses—The Census Bureau provides the annual County Business Patterns (CBP) series of economic data. Included is number of recreation business establishments, payroll, and number of employees for the full range of businesses as described in the North American Industry Classification System. Nine of the business classes listed are related to outdoor recreation. Summarized in this report are number of business establishments per capita, along with percentage change from the 1998 to the 2007.

County Pattern Maps—Included in this report are county-level maps for 2008 that depict patterns of recreation resource availability per capita across northern counties and the rest of the Nation. (These recreation resource maps employ the same criteria as was used with the demographic data, which displays four shading levels based on percentage distributions of the data: 0 to 35, 36 to 70, 71 to 90, and 91 to 100.) Recreation resources per capita within a 75-mile radius of each county are displayed in the maps.

The 75-mile zone includes a home county plus all surrounding counties whose geographic centers or centroids are within a 75-mile straight-line distance from the home county centroid. This distance is roughly the equivalent of a recreation day trip. The three basic recreation resources summarized in this report are combined Federal land and State park area, non-Federal forest land, and water area (from census Tiger geographic data).

PROJECTED FUTURES

Using the population projections described earlier, projections of per capita recreation resources were developed for three resources. The projection index used is the ratio of per capita acres predicted for 2060 relative to the per capita acres that existed in base year 2008. This statistic indicates the percent of the resource currently available per capita that is forecast to remain by 2060. The per capita future is forecast for three recreation resources—Federal and State parkland, non-Federal forest land, and water. Projections are summarized for the North and for other regions. Also reported is the percentage of total surface area in each region represented by the resource.

Literature Cited

Cordell, H.K. 2008. The latest on trends in nature-based outdoor recreation. Forest History Today. Spring: 4-10.

U.S. Department of Agriculture Forest Service. 2009a. National survey on recreation and the environment [NSRE Dataset]. On file with: U.S. Department of Agriculture Forest Service, Southern Research Station, Recreation, Wilderness, Urban Forest, and Demographic Trends Research Group, 320 Green St., Athens, GA 30602-2044.

U.S. Department of Commerce, Census Bureau. 2009a. SC-EST2009-alldata6: annual state resident population estimates for 6 race groups (5 race alone groups and one group with two or more race groups) by age, sex, and Hispanic origin: April 1, 2000 to July 1, 2009. http://www.census.gov/compendia/statab/2011/tables/11s0019.xls. (9 January 2012).

U.S. Department of Commerce, Census Bureau. 2009b. CC-EST2009-ALLDATA-[ST-FIPS]: annual county resident population estimates by age, sex, race, and Hispanic origin: April 1, 2000 to July 1, 2009. http://www.census.gov/popest/data/counties/asrh/2009/CC-EST2009-alldata.html. (9 January 2012).

Woods & Poole Economics, Inc. 2009. 2010 complete economic and demographic data source (CEDDS) .Washington, DC. Woods & Poole Economics, Inc. [CD-ROM].

Zarnoch, S.J.; Cordell, H.K.; Betz, C.J.; Bergstrom, J.C. 2010. Multiple imputation: an application to income nonresponse in the national survey on recreation and the environment. Res. Pap. SRS–49. Asheville, NC: U.S. Department of Agriculture Forest Service, Southern Research Station. 15 p.

A B S T R A C T

In the last two decades, the North's population grew at a considerably slower rate than the Nation as a whole. Nevertheless, this region's population is large and in all likelihood will continue to grow. This means greater development of land and water resources at the same time that there is growth in demand for outdoor recreation. This report looks at recent population trends and forecasts within the context of other U.S. regions, demographic composition of population, recreation participation by residents age 16 and older, trends in activities and time spent outdoors by its youth, and the changes occurring in recreation resources, both public and private. The region referenced here includes the area within the corner States of Maine, Minnesota, Missouri, and Maryland. Much of the research reported here ties to data, analyses, and findings developed for the U.S. Department of Agriculture Forest Service 2010 Renewable Resources Planning Act (RPA) Assessment (Cordell 2012) and how they affect the sustainability of northern forests.

Keywords: trends, population, outdoor recreation, natural resources, northern United States